Information Governance
for
Executives

First Edition

Contact us at IGTraining.com for bulk book orders and custom branding opportunities. Order individual copies of this book at **Amazon.com**

Thank you to Richard and Dennis Kessler (not related, actually!) for their fine contributions, which added to the book. I would also like to gratefully acknowledge Mark Grysiuk for his editing and contributions to this book. He took it on at a very busy time!

Bacchus Business Books
San Diego, USA

Library of Congress Cataloguing-in-Publication Data:

Smallwood, Robert F., 1959-
Information Governance for Executives: Fundamentals and Strategies/ Robert F. Smallwood
Includes bibliographical references and index.

ISBN 978-1530475100
ISBN 1530475104

Information technology—Management. 2. Management Information Systems. 3. Electronic records—Management. I. Title

Printed in the United States of America. First Printings: April 2016.

IG for Executives

For Jim Minihan

Robert Smallwood

Information Governance for Executives

Fundamentals and Strategies

ROBERT F. SMALLWOOD

Robert F. Smallwood is also the author of several key books on information governance: *Information Governance* (Wiley, 2014), *Managing Electronic Records* (Wiley, 2013), *Safeguarding Critical E-documents* (Wiley, 2012), and *Taming the Email Tiger* (Bacchus Business, 2008).

Robert Smallwood

CONTENTS

7

Robert Smallwood

INTRODUCTION

How this Book Will Help You Implement IG Successfully

Information governance (IG) is increasingly seen as a critical initiative in well–run organizations. IG is about minimizing information risks and costs while maximizing its value. IG is, in short, the ability to secure, control and optimize information. But IG has often been presented as a complicated and blurry concept, and IG programs have often fallen short of their aims.

This book will provide you with crystal-clear definitions of IG and its concepts, give you a high-level understanding of the drivers and benefits of IG, help you develop the business case, and show you how to launch and manage an ongoing IG program. You will also benefit from proven IG program strategies and advice offered by leading IG practitioners.

Robert Smallwood

Part I

Introduction to IG

Robert Smallwood

Chapter 1

What is Information Governance?

Many executives are somewhat confused about the definition of information governance (IG).

IG has suffered through dozens of definitions, some errant and some fabulously verbose, causing IG to become a foggy and often misunderstood concept.

This book will simplify the definitions, concepts, and strategies for you so that they are clear and solidly a part of your management approach.

Information governance is about *minimizing information risks and costs and maximizing its value.*

Succinctly, IG is, **"security, control, and optimization** of information."

This is a definition anyone can remember. Let's break it down a little.

This definition means that information—particularly confidential, personal, or other sensitive information—is kept **secure** in its three states: at rest, in transit, and in use.

It means that your organizational IG processes **control** *who* has access to *which* information, and *when.*

And it means that information that no longer has business value is destroyed and the most valuable information is leveraged to provide new insights and value. In other words, it is **optimized**.

To round out your understanding of the reach and impact of IG, a more detailed definition is, "policy-based control of information to maximize value and meet legal, regulatory, risk, and business demands." Because IG is about being able to consistently provide the proper information to meet these demands.

What all the definitions are getting at is what it means to *govern* information, as opposed to leaving it uncontrolled and unprotected, and allowing it to spiral out of control.

We have seen the consequences of this, with colossal IG failures that almost daily expose major corporations to reputational and financial risk. Like the **Sony Pictures** and **Anthem Health** breaches in 2014 and 2015. These companies obviously did not know where all their personally identifiable information (PII), protected health information (PHI), and confidential electronic documents were located and took no extra measures to secure that valuable information.[1]

They—and most major corporations—are not managing information as an asset, and do not have a current accounting of their information assets. That is, there is no information inventory or "data map" of where different types of information are stored and they would have difficulty finding all incidences of it so that it may be secured.

Most organizations are not paying attention: they leave sensitive information out there floating around on their servers unsecured, unencrypted. When it comes time to attend to the problem, most often they "kick the can down the road" and do nothing.

The consequences only become clear after a major event like a data breach, which can result in thousands of customers and employees being dragged into a "life long battle" to control their personal information. Or the realization may come when a major lawsuit causes runaway legal costs or a significant or fine or sanction is levied.

Let's face it: *perimeter security of most networks is easily breached.* So sensitive and confidential information must be identified, secured, tracked, and controlled. That means an IG program must be in place with the formal policies and procedures necessary to govern information assets. And that program will also help an organization meet compliance and legal demands while improving the quality of information provided to managers for decision-making. It's win-win-win all around but it is also a major undertaking that requires a commitment to the long haul.

IG Programs Are About Enforcing Policy Consistently

Standardized and systematized IG policy means that information is identified (mapped) and **classified**, and, if justified, protected with security technologies like **encryption**.

IG also means that **vital records**—those which the business absolutely must have to continue operations in the event of a disaster—are identified and safeguarded properly.

Practicing good IG means managing the information lifecycle: that information is kept as long as required by regulations and statutes, and internal business needs, and then it is discarded according to an established retention and disposition schedule, (unless it is subject to a legal hold during litigation).

When you are keeping your information asset stores cleaned up, there are ongoing benefits. Not just lower operating costs and improved productivity, but also the information that remains is higher-value to the business and can be leveraged to create new insights that feed into management decisions. This can provide a strategic advantage.

Don't Confuse Simple Data Governance with Information Governance

Data governance and information governance are often confused.

They are distinct disciplines, but data governance is a subset of IG, and should be a part of an overall IG program. We are going to get just a bit technical here, so bear with us. We will break it down for you: Data governance entails maintaining clean, unique (non-duplicate), structured data (in databases). Structured data is typically about 10% of the total amount of information stored in an organization. Often, a formal Chief Data Officer (CDO) who deals with data privacy, security, quality, and governance oversees data governance.

Data governance includes data modeling and data security, and also involves data cleansing (or data scrubbing) to strip out corrupted, inaccurate, or extraneous data and de-duplication, to eliminate redundant occurrences of data. Data governance focuses on *data quality* from the ground up at the lowest or root level, so that subsequent reports, analyses, and conclusions are based on clean, reliable, trusted data in database tables. Data governance is the most rudimentary level to implement IG.

The Challenge: Managing Unstructured Information

Unstructured information is the roughly 90% of information that organizations struggle to manage which includes email messages, word processing documents, PDF documents, presentation slides, spreadsheets, scanned images, and the like. Unstructured information is more challenging to manage than structured information in databases, and is the primary focus of IG programs. Unstructured information generally lacks detailed metadata to describe its contents. Methodically adding metadata to unstructured information helps you to categorize and manage it. There are software tools to assist in this effort.

IG is much more broad than data governance and consists of the overarching polices and processes to optimize and leverage information while keeping it secure and meeting legal and privacy obligations in alignment with stated organizational business objectives.

IG Requires Cross-functional Collaboration

IG is a new, maturing discipline that most organizations have not yet begun to tackle due to its complexity and cross-functional nature. It involves information security (infosec), privacy, legal issues, IT, risk management, records management functions and more. It is a complex beast with lots of arms and legs.

IG must be driven from the top down by a strong executive sponsor, with day-to-day management by an IG lead, possibly a formal "Chief IG Officer" orchestrating the activities of an IG steering committee.

IG programs are often aimed at reducing legal costs and information risk. These are big targets. However, the payoff can be huge, not only in cost reduction but in reducing information (and reputational) risk.

Just ask Anthem or Sony Pictures.

* * * * *

The Facets of Information Governance

The IG Initiative released its 2015-16 report on the state of the information governance (IG) industry. IG professionals were surveyed for a second year in a row and the results show a market that is maturing, and coming into focus.

Of note is the comparison of the "facets of IG" from 2014 to 2015-16, which stayed largely the same. That means consensus is building as to IG's identity, and the market is solidifying. Looking at the graphic below, the top facets, or functional areas of IG are:

1. Records and Information Management (RIM)
2. Information Security
3. Compliance
4. E-discovery
5. Data governance
6. Privacy
7. Risk management
8. Data storage and archiving

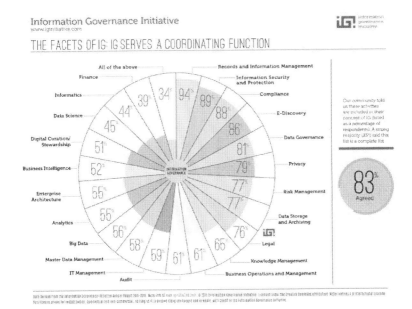

So you can see how far-reaching IG programs are – spanning across a variety of functional groups. This is what makes IG efforts so challenging: they require collaboration across these various groups, which will have varying agendas, as well as individual personalities. So it is the executive sponsor's job to get them to focus on business objectives which will benefit the organization as a whole.

Focusing on discrete IG-related projects within your IG program will help to maintain focus and allow your organization to move forward accruing the benefits of IG.

- **IG is about minimizing information risks and costs while maximizing its value.**
- IG is, "security, control, & optimization of information."
- Data governance focuses on getting clean data into databases and is a subset of IG
- Perimeter security of most networks is easily breached. So sensitive and confidential information must be identified, secured, tracked, and controlled.
- IG means managing the information lifecycle.
- IG is cross-functional in nature.
- IG must be driven from the top down by a strong executive sponsor
- Key facets of IG include: Records and Information Management (RIM), Information Security, Compliance, E-discovery, Data governance, Privacy, Risk management.

Chapter 2

Why Information Governance?

Big Data is Here and Only Getting Bigger

According to the research firm IDC, the digital universe is doubling in size every two years, and will reach 44 trillion gigabytes by 2020. Estimates and projections vary, but it has been stated that 90 percent of the data existing worldwide today was created in the last two years and that every two days more information is generated than was from the dawn of civilization until 2003. That's a lot of information.

This trend will continue and all that Big Data piling up has real costs for organizations: The burden of massive stores of information has increased storage costs dramatically, caused overloaded systems to fail, and increased legal discovery costs. Further, the longer that data is kept, the more likely that it will need to be migrated to newer computing platforms. This drives up conversion costs and brings chain of custody issues into question in legal matters; and also, there is the risk that somewhere in that mountain of data an organization stores is a piece of information that represents a significant legal liability.

What is Big Data exactly? It is a volume and velocity of data that is not able to be managed with today's commercial database tools. Too big to manage. However, there are golden needles in that mounting haystack.

21

In today's information overload era of Big Data the ability to distill key insights from enormous amounts of data is a major business differentiator and source of sustainable competitive advantage. In fact, a report by the World Economic Forum stated that data is a new asset class and personal data is "the new oil." And we are generating more data than we can manage effectively with current methods and tools.

Organizations that are able to efficiently dispose of "data debris" return more profit to shareholders, reduce their legal exposure, and are able to make more strategic investments in IT.

Organizations have to get rid of some of that irrelevant information sludge to find the gold—much of the information they are managing has no business value and can be characterized as **redundant, outdated, or trivial** (ROT) information. You'll see the term "ROT" used throughout this book, and you'll hear it used in IG presentations. ROT is simply garbage information or data debris that has no value.

However, most all organizations are managing that ROT with the same high-value IT and management resources that they use to manage information that has real business value. This is clearly a waste and misapplication of resources. An avoidable waste.

According to a survey taken at a Compliance, Governance and Oversight Counsel (CGOC) summit, respondents estimated that approximately 25 percent of information stored in organizations has real business value.[2]

Let that soak in: *only* about one-quarter of the information organizations are managing has business value*!*

Even if this estimate is *way off* it would be a stunning number if it were only found that half of the information being managed has real value. It is mind-boggling just how inefficient organizations are at governing their information assets. Imagine if you managed your financial assets in such a way!

According to the CGOC study, another five percent of information must be kept as business records and about one percent is retained due to a litigation hold. So based on their estimates, roughly 69% of information stored and managed by organizations has no business, legal, or regulatory value.

That means that more than 2/3 of the information organizations store has no value. If their estimates are wildly inaccurate, this should still cause alarm for executives. *Even if 1/2 or 1/3 of your information has no value then your organization is running terribly inefficiently!*

Time to clean house. Enter Information Governance.

What will IG do for your company? "The hallmark of IG is managing information effectively and efficiently to gain the greatest advantage possible while protecting against negative exposure."[3]

An IG program that manages the security, control, retention, and disposal of information and focuses on legally defensible deletion can return tangible benefits to stakeholders—and stockholders.

Fewer disk drives, fewer tapes, fewer data center operations employees, slower growth in power needs, and reduced e-discovery collection and review costs are some of the hard cost savings.

At the same time better, cleaner, more accurate information can be provided to knowledge workers to use as a basis for their decisions. This will improve decision quality, and also, they will be able to find that information faster which yields productivity benefits—less time searching for information, more time working.

With a smaller information footprint, organizations can more easily find what they need and derive business value from it.

Further, with IG you reduce your legal risk, since electronically stored information (ESI) that is discarded in a systematic way according to policy cannot be requested in legal proceedings. That is, so long as the policy is standardized, reasonable, and uniformly followed. Moreover, since the organization will organize and manage its information in a proactive way it can more quickly and completely implement legal holds and find the information that is responsive to a particular legal proceeding. Organizations must eliminate the constantly-accumulating data debris regularly and consistently, and to do this, processes and systems must be in place to cull out valuable information and discard the data debris. An IG program sets the framework to accomplish this. Then it takes a sustained and focused effort to continue to reap benefits.

Why the "Keep Everything Forever" Approach Is Not Viable

Some executives think that storage is cheap and with the cloud even cheaper so why not just keep everything, so it is there when you need it? Therefore, you do not risk deleting something that may be important in the future? This premise has caused a debate in the IG community.

Those on one side contend that we are moving to a world where we retain all information—forever. No need to identify ROT information and weed it out. Not worth it, they argue.

Some even contend that IG is just a fad and advances in search technology will soon eliminate the need for IG. The arguments go something like this:

1) Yesterday's trash may be tomorrow's treasure: We won't know what data has value until well into the future. Today, we do not have the construct to understand what relevant insights, patterns, or trends may be hidden in the data that, as business conditions change, may be valuable in the future;

2) We don't want to get caught deleting something that regulators or superiors may look for in the future;

3) It is time-consuming, expensive, and politically charged to attempt to delete large collections or categories of data, e-documents and information, and, just not worth the effort from an ROI standpoint;

4) The cost of storage is effectively being driven down to zero with cloud offerings that offer low-cost storage upfront, and big companies like Microsoft, Apple and Google will win this argument in the marketplace;

5) Search technologies will be so good in a few years that classifying information and having a metadata strategy in place is pointless.

On their face, the arguments seem to come together. Things are going that way and technology trends are making it easier to keep everything forever, so why put in the effort?

The argument holds up until it is brought out from the shadows of the theoretical to the realities of conducting business and day-to-day operations.

Here is why you cannot keep storing all your information indefinitely, from a practical management standpoint:

25

1) Culture — For executive management, the "keep everything" paradigm sets a poor professional tone in an organization. Retaining all information—no matter how useless—does not make business sense. Why would you keep copies of copies, copies that are renamed, empty spreadsheet or word processing files, temporary log files, personal emails, illicit files like personal pictures, music, and video and the rest of the worthless information filling up storage space? Yesterday's trash is tomorrow's trash. And it sets a bad example. It says that your organization is willing to just add storage, suffer sanctions, lose lawsuits, and pay huge fines rather than deal with IG issues. Not focusing on policies and rules for governing information encourages a sloppy operational culture fraught with inefficiencies. It is the opposite of what leading organizations strive for: continued improvements in operational efficiency. In a recent report by **Osterman Research**, almost half of organizations studied cited "employee productivity" as a driver for IG efforts.

2) Poor data quality — "Garbage in equals garbage out." Data scientists cannot extract accurate and valuable insights without clean, non-duplicated data. In fact, they are being overwhelmed with messy big data, and in a recent survey of data scientists:

> *"2/3 of data scientists surveyed stated that cleaning and organizing data is the least interesting and most time-consuming task in their jobs."*

So sending a bunch of data filled with junk to your data science team will decrease their productivity, skew and invalidate results, and aggravate them. It creates a poor work environment, which also relates to the culture.

Further, a dose of reality: Carl Thomas, the IG lead at JPMorganChase stated that during their IG efforts when they dug down deep into their business units, the number one comment or complaint they found was business managers unsure of, or dissatisfied with, *information quality.* Managers generally did not have confidence in the underlying information used as a basis for decisions—and this is within the highly-automated, controlled, and managed environment of a market leader!

In addition, various studies from leading research firms confirm this to be widely true: that a significant percentage of information (~25%+) in organizations is flawed—IG efforts work to improve information quality.

3) Cost – first off you have soaring e-discovery and regulatory costs. These are real. When digital information is not well-organized or easily found, it adds greatly to the costs of e-discovery collection and review, and meeting regulatory demands. The processes are costly and labor-intensive, rather than streamlined, repeatable, routine, and automated. Also, when, on average, 40%-70% of information most organizations are storing is duplicate, then that is wasting resources that could go to the bottom line or be invested elsewhere. One client we have spends $40M/year on digital storage and it is increasing by 40% per year. Cleaning up what they have can cut storage needs. Even stemming this growth will save hard dollars in the future.

"Freedom ain't free. And neither is storage."

What many cloud providers are doing is simply cost-shifting, otherwise known as the old "bait and switch" in the used car sales world. They are cutting the price they charge for storage but making it up on the back end by charging for analytics and other services when you need to access that information. They are willing to take losses to gain market share, although later they will be under pressure to earn a profit for shareholders. Nevertheless, if your organization is going the cloud route, cleaner, unique (de-duplicated) information as a result of your IG program means less cost as many enterprise storage providers charge per gigabyte.

To be sure: Regardless of pricing model, digital storage operations have hard costs. There are servers, disk drives, optical units, controllers, cables, tapes, software (master data management, file management, compression, security, etc.) and such, and it all has to be housed in a secure, air-conditioned facility with raised flooring. There are labor costs associated with storage operations and the hardware and software must be serviced and maintained.

Beware of cloud providers that offer nearly "free" storage—once they have most all your digital content, what is to keep them from changing their business model in a few years and holding your information hostage? Has any organization experienced this phenomenon when they sent boxes upon boxes of paper files off to be stored in a warehouse for a cheap upfront fee? Isn't it strange how the complicated storage and retrieval fees add up over time? The same thing can happen in the digital world. Only the consequences will be worse. Your organization will not be able to very easily or cheaply migrate all that information over to a competitive cloud provider once it is housed in a cloud repository. The tools to accomplish this are not the available today. And it is not in your cloud provider's interest: they have no business motivation to make it easy for you to leave. You are locked in.

4) Risk – The Sedona Commentary on Information Governance states, "Regardless of an individual organization's size, mission, marketplace or industry, information is a crucial asset for all organizations and, if inadequately controlled, a dangerous source of risk and liability." That is a pretty clear statement. And reality proves it out.

Our consulting firm recently worked with a large financial institution that estimated their risk of poor IG to be in excess of $1B, due to the fines and sanctions in excess of that amount that had been imposed on some of their competitors. So there are real compliance and legal risks that add up to costs for not having set processes in place to consistently and systematically govern information. These are largely avoidable costs.

Another standard argument for defensible deletion is avoiding litigation risk. If your organization has processes in place to systematically and consistently delete information (mostly we are talking about email messages here) that is not on legal hold or likely to be, or not a record or likely to become one, then potentially damaging information may be routinely discarded according to schedule. It is not discoverable and no sanctions or adverse inferences can be handed down if a documented and standardized process for defensible deletion is in place and followed routinely. Your lawyers should like this. But often they want to keep everything forever, "to be on the safe side."

There is also the ever-present risk of data breaches. When your organization is not striving for operational efficiency and continuing to improve its governance of information, it is not taking all the steps it can to protect the privacy of personal information that is in its possession, which could be revealed in the breach. A breach will cost the organization money, employees, customers, brand equity. Like what happened to Sony Pictures. Or Target. Or Anthem, and so on. Without a consistent IG program, the organization is not protecting its reputation and brand in the event of a breach as well as it could, which may be looked on as negligent or at least irresponsible by shareholders and customers.

And there is a third option between full retention and complete (legally defensible) deletion if the organization is cost-conscious yet concerned about complete deletion: deleting the unstructured information but retaining the metadata derived from its content. Metadata is summary in nature. This approach will also support leveraging analytics to create new information value in the future in that good clean metadata (which includes who authorized the destruction) can be used in future analyses.

5) Privacy – European countries and many U.S. states (with more to follow) have enacted legislation requiring that organizations, after a set period of time, must delete and completely discard personal information (PII, PHI, PCI) once the transactions that required that information have been completed. This means that the organization must take IG steps like creating a data map and information asset register to know where personal information resides so they can protect it and delete it according to schedule. Further, to reduce the risk of breaches, that personal information should be locked down with encryption, rights management, and redaction technologies, to protect it in the event of a breach.

So, a practical IG program will have built-in, formalized, repeatable and "routinized" processes for governing information on an ongoing basis. This includes deleting data debris and information that has lost its value.

Overall, these recommendations will help foster processes that yield better, cleaner information for analytics to be used as a basis for decision-making, allow for more efficient and cost-effective processes in meeting legal and regulatory demands, and support a culture of compliance and operational efficiency.

Attacking the Old "Silo" Approach

IG Programs also help to break down siloed approaches to organizational problem solving that have been traditionally driven vertically down through functional groups. This approach does not account for business needs across various functions (e.g. legal, privacy, security, compliance, risk management), and does not leverage multi-disciplinary efforts. Resources are wasted and these approaches have proven to be ineffective.

To give you a better feel for the "future state" of what an IG-proficient organization looks like, a review of the major benefits of IG programs are listed below, (from Baron & Marcos):

"An IG program enables companies to achieve, for example:

✓ Comprehensive, streamlined approaches to business policies and processes affecting information.

✓ Collaboration within and across business functions to address institutional data [information] challenges.

✓ Clear decision-making processes that promote enterprise wide strategic planning. [See Chapter 10, Strategic Planning and Best Practices.]

✓ More efficient use of organizational resources dedicated to records and information management (RIM), data privacy, information security and litigation responses.

✓ Greater use of automation to streamline workflows and reduce bureaucratic burdens on end-users.

✓ A better holistic understanding of company data [information].

✓ A dedicated business function focused on the analytical capabilities and opportunities available to extract business value from company information.

✓ A dedicated infrastructure that is ready to respond to incidents regarding the improper disclosure or management of company information.

Additionally, IG guards against:

✓ Potential liability stemming from inconsistent company policies and processes regarding data management.

- ✓ Siloed approaches to resolving institutional challenges, which do not account for the needs of all business stakeholders and ultimately waste enterprise resources.

- ✓ Failures to properly escalate serious issues that require executive-level attention.

- ✓ Bad actors within the organization that threaten the company's security and reputation.

- ✓ Unidentified deficiencies in company practices regarding RIM, data privacy, information security and litigation responses.

- ✓ The accumulation of vast amounts of legacy data of questionable value."[4]

You can see the benefits of strong IG programs can be significant and far-reaching across the entire organization.

Major IG Failures

Here are two examples of IG failures, which were very public. These bring IG weaknesses fully into view.

Case Brief #1

An Information Governance Failure: Chipotle Mexican Grill's Foodborne Illness Outbreaks

The goal that Chipotle Mexican Grill strives for is: to serve "food with integrity" that is fresh, not GMO, and never frozen. It is their corporate mantra. This is why the reports in 2015 of foodborne illnesses at some Chipotle stores were so damning. And the stock and market value reflected this, dropping over 40% in only three months. That's around $5 billion in value that has vanished due to the reputational damage wrought on the Chipotle brand. That is huge.

If only they'd had a good IG program in place, all of that loss could have been avoided.

There were reports that the food poisonings may be the result of industrial espionage, and they may well be true. The FBI opened an investigation. Multiple parties have benefited from Chipotle's losses. A hedge fund manager shorting the stock may have raked in billions (hint to investigators—check on all the short bets). Competitors have improved their market standing during Chipotle's losses. In addition, even some alternative (traditional) suppliers have gained ground:

> "Market Watch wrote that the result of all of these outbreaks will be to force Chipotle to obtain their produce from larger corporate farms that can afford the more extensive microbial food-safety testing programs and to process vegetables at centralized locations instead of at the individual stores, both of which are industry-standard practices that the company had previously criticized."[143]

And what is the crux of the matter? Information risk coming home to roost, from poor IG.

Chipotle managers did not have the proper level of detailed information to track exactly where in their supply chain their ingredients had been contaminated, which is a result of weaknesses in their IG and recordkeeping practices.

"It also has been pointed out that Chipotle's current **record-keeping** system is actually hindering the health authorities' investigation in locating the sources of the various infections."[144]

No deaths occurred, but people got sick and the Chipotle brand suffered a major hit. All of that could have been prevented not only with improved food quality testing, but the detailed tracking of ingredient lot numbers. The fact that this information was not available to Chipotle managers was the result of a failure to construct proper records and information management (RIM) systems. It is a failure in IG.

Case Brief #2

Sony Pictures Breach: Info-terrorism that Could Have Been Prevented

The Sony Pictures data breach in late 2014 revealed vast amounts of confidential information to the public. Not only were unreleased films exposed, but also strategic marketing plans, detailed internal cost models, industry salary comparisons, termination and/or severance information, confidential email messages, email addresses and passwords, and even employees' PII, including the social security numbers, birthdates, salaries, and performance reviews of all 3,800+ employees.

The "Guardians of Peace" hackers aim was ostensibly (and perhaps it was simple misdirection) to stop the release of "The Interview," a satiric movie about the assassination of North Korea's dictator Kim Jong Un. Estimates state the damage to the company as being in the $100 million range.

They are likely way off. If calculable, ultimately, the damage could exceed $1B to Sony in lost revenue, I.T. security costs, cyber-insurance costs, missed opportunities, employee turnover and hiring, reputational ill will, and perhaps other areas that have not yet been identified.[5]

The negative economic impact will go on for years.

Because, for one, even though Sony will try to cover the costs of identity theft for its employees, that lingering liability will be out there for years and years for those people. Their personal information is out there for the world to see. Certainly the credit card companies, banks, and credit bureaus will assist in the mitigation effort, but people whose PII has been revealed publicly can't change their birth date and changing their social security number or even name will take months, and involve voluminous paperwork. Rogue organizations that did not participate in the initial cyber-attack may attempt to capitalize on the breached PII right away or once things have cooled down months or years later.

Also, Sony Pictures' competitors now have keen insights into Sony's internal operating cost models and business plans. So Sony will not only move to counter those plans, but also, they will have to change some of them to less optimal approaches, due to the exposure of their strategies. Further, Sony competitors will easily be able to poach talent by simply offering a more secure and new work environment. Sony recruitment efforts will be more costly, and they will incur hiring, onboarding and training costs they would not have if not for the data breach, and breach of employees' trust.

In addition, there may be more breached information that hackers accessed and are selling on the black market or they have yet to release.

What could have saved Sony—even after the breach? Information governance.

Even after the successful cyber-attack, proper IG controls and enabling technologies would have kept confidential information secure. But beyond that, it would have mitigated the reputational damage that was suffered when key Sony executives were exposed disparaging the talents of major stars like Angelina Jolie, Adam Sandler, and others.

Just exactly how could an IG program have helped?

IG is more than cyber security, which obviously failed in this case. It is obvious that perimeter security does not work well. Any organization can be hacked, and the larger they are, often the easier it is.

In short, IG means not only security of information but also control of it, and that means knowing what data you have, where it resides, and protecting it, especially confidential information assets and PII. Control means controlling not just the information stored in systems, but controlling information that gets in to the systems, and then who has access to that information after the fact.

So, if Sony's email policy would have stated, in part, "No insults or personally disparaging information about our employees, suppliers, contractors, or potential business partners may be stated in email or other messaging services provided by the Company," they would have been much better off. But you have to go further. There must be clear penalties for violating company policy, including demotion, pay cuts, suspension, or termination. If Sony had done this then executives would have been discouraged from making such statements in writing on the company's email messaging system in the first place.

Too bad they didn't have that policy in place. Too bad they didn't monitor and audit it. Too bad the CEO was asleep at the wheel and did not activate an IG initiative within the company.

The Sony incident opens up a Pandora's Box for managers and shareholders; future attacks and blackmail schemes will come, and other organizations will be hit. Only next time they may demand money, bitcoins, weapons, hostages, or changes in corporate (or even governmental) policy. Rogue attackers now know they can bring a large corporation to its knees. Large corporations with deep pockets are focused on quarterly profits, and procrastinating when it comes to implementing IG programs. The resulting weakness was exposed when Sony caved in pretty fast.

IG could have saved Sony Pictures a lot of embarrassment and expense. Now they will pay economic and reputational risk costs for years as they attempt to clean up the mess. Moreover, they have made a nice business case for IG, which will be studied in business schools in the coming decade.

We can see the impact of management's failure to address these obvious IG risks, as made quite clear with the revelations of the Sony Pictures breach.

Will your organization be next?

CHAPTER SUMMARY: KEY POINTS

- **Organizations that are able to efficiently dispose of "data debris" return more profit to shareholders and reduce legal liabilities.**
- In today's Big Data era, the digital universe is doubling in size every two years.
- "ROT" is redundant, outdated, and trivial information.
- Most organizations manage ROT with the same high-value resources as high-value information.
- Only about 25% of information most organizations manage has business value.
- With a smaller information footprint, organizations can more easily find what they need and derive business value from it.
- Keeping all information "forever" is untenable due to cost, risk, and legal issues.
- IG programs manage information effectively and efficiently while protecting against negative exposure.[6]
- IG policies and technologies can secure your confidential information even after a breach.

Chapter 3

Who Should Be Part of an Information Governance Program?

Implementing IG programs **requires a cross-functional approach.** IG has a wide reach and effective IG brings together stakeholders from across the organization and leverages their synergies to better govern and optimize information.

Due to the expanse of an IG program, your IG program team or steering committee should be set up with a tiered structure. The core departments driving your IG program, or "top tier" should be:[7]

- **Legal.** Because legal considerations trump all others, your legal department must be deeply involved in the IG effort, best represented by your General Counsel, Assistant GC, or a senior legal officer. In addition, legal costs and liabilities can soar with poor IG, further underscoring the importance of efficient legal functions. Further, Legal must implement "litigation response protocols" and drive e-discovery efforts—which inherently involve IT and records management policies, two other core stakeholders in IG programs. Your legal department also must provide opinions on privacy matters to ensure compliance;

- **Information technology**. IT is key to IG efforts. You will be leveraging IT to improve efficiencies and monitor the effectiveness of your IG program. Also, IT must work with

Legal and RIM to preserve the organization's electronically stored information (ESI) in legal matters;

- **Records management** (or records and information management, RIM). Your RIM department is responsible for maintaining corporate records to ensure compliance with "applicable statutory and regulatory requirements." RIM must also work with Legal to execute e-discovery functions;

- **Information security.** "InfoSec" is responsible for keeping your databases and confidential information secure, and providing policy input to prevent the loss of intellectual property (IP). InfoSec has played an increasingly greater role in IG programs due to colossal data breaches, privacy concerns, and reputational risk;

- **Privacy.** Your Privacy group must conduct research and provide policy guidance for the handling of personally identifiable information (PII), protected health information (PHI), and other sensitive customer and employee information. The goal is to have privacy considerations "baked in" to your everyday processes, so that you achieve, "privacy by design." [8]This is a core aim of IG programs.

So your core IG steering committee group must include Legal, IT, RIM, InfoSec, and Privacy, if you have those groups represented in your organizational structure. Moreover, there is precedent for this, when looking at the Information Governance Reference Model (IGRM). The IGRM is a simple tool to graphically display the key impact areas of IG programs to spur discussion of IG's cross-functional nature (source: EDRM.net).

Information Governance Reference Model (IGRM)

Linking duty + value to information asset = efficient, effective management

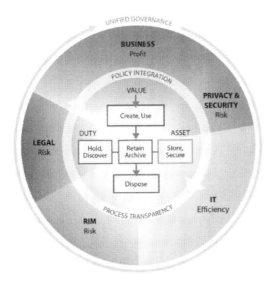

Duty: Legal obligation for specific information

Value: Utility or business purpose of specific information

Asset: Specific container of information

Information Governance Reference Model / © 2012 / v3.0 / edrm.net

You will notice that there is one more group depicted, "Business" or business units. The key business unit(s) you may want to include in your IG program will vary based on your organizational structure and business scenario. Business units provide critical input in your IG policy development efforts.

Some additional critical departments that should be represented on the next tier of your IG steering committee, depending on your organizational structure and business scenario, may be:

- **Risk Management.** Managing information risk is core to IG efforts. You can see "Risk" noted as a focus in the IGRM graphic under "Legal," "Privacy & Security," and "RIM." If you have a formal risk management department their involvement in the IG program will be valuable;

- **Compliance**. Large organizations and those in highly regulated entities may have a formal Compliance function. Compliance efforts focus both externally regarding regulations and statutory requirements, and internally to ensure employees follow company policies and procedures, as well as externally imposed requirements;

- **Human Resources**. HR is central to your communications and training strategy to help embed IG considerations like privacy and security into routine business processes. Emphasizing compliance with IG policies and procedures in employee performance reviews will involve working with HR to develop meaningful metrics;

- **Audit.** Your Audit department can play a key role in measuring your progress based on meaningful metrics, and providing feedback for improvement. Audit findings can provide crucial input for decision-making within your IG program;

- **Change Management** (CM). If you have a formal CM function, they can play a key role, as all IG programs are fundamentally CM efforts. Often an external consultant can assist in developing your CM plan to complement IG efforts;

- **Analytics.** "To the extent an organization relies on data analytics to enhance products, services or business offerings, the analytics function drives the strategic direction of an IG program. Harnessing the value of information is one of the foundational purposes of IG, but an IG program also must balance the goals of analytics against information risks and retention requirements."[9]

Assigning Team Roles and Responsibilities

The executive sponsor must designate an IG program manager, and depending on the focus of the IG effort, that person could come from one of several areas including legal, infosec, risk management, records management, or IT.

In terms of breaking down the roles and responsibilities of the remainder of the IG team, the easy decision is to have IG team representatives take responsibility for the functional areas of their expertise. Nevertheless, there will be overlap, and it is best to have some pairs or small workgroups teamed up to gain the broadest amount of input and optimum results.

This will also facilitate cross-training. For instance, inside legal counsel may be responsible for rendering the final legal opinions, but not being an expert in records or document management or risk management means they could benefit from input of others in specialized functional areas, which will inform them and help narrow and focus their legal research. So when performing the basic research as to which regulations and laws apply to the organization regarding security, retention, and preservation of email, e-records, and PII, the initial research could be conducted by the SRO or records management head, in consultation with the corporate archivist and CIO, with the results of their findings and recommendations drafted and sent to the legal counsel. The draft report may offer up several alternative approaches that need legal input and decisions. Then the legal department can conduct their own, focused research, and make final recommendations in consideration of the organization's legal strategy, business objectives, financial position, and applicable laws and regulations.

The result of the research, consultation, and collaboration of the IG team should result in a final draft of the IG strategic plan (see

Chapter 10 for more detail). It will still need more input and development to align the plan with business objectives, an analysis of internal and external drivers, applicable best practices, competitive analysis, applicable information technology trends, an analysis and inclusion of the organization's culture, and other factors.

Caveat: The Importance of Tiering Your IG Steering Committee

If you look over some of the research and anecdotal observations on IG programs you will find that often IG efforts are slow to start, and they get put on hold, and re-start, and maybe the effort is abandoned. Then later, it dawns on executives that the "IG problem" (e.g. non-compliance fines and sanctions, soaring litigation costs, risks of colossal information breaches, failure to capitalize on emerging opportunities by leveraging analytics) isn't going away so they re-start again.

One of the root causes of sluggish IG efforts is the basic failure to structure the IG steering committee properly, and to consider the realities of group dynamics, corporate politics, scheduling, and program management.

Since IG efforts are by nature cross-functional and require the involvement of key stakeholder groups, your IG steering committee can become large and unwieldy and the politics can become crippling, causing progress to slow and threatening the continuation of the IG program.

In practice we have seen IG steering committees of 15, 18, even 20 individuals representing the various functional groups. There may be a clear executive sponsor at some point early on but when that person realizes they will be held accountable for the performance of groups outside their direct control (and competitors at their corporate level can then sabotage progress), they often look for cover and find a way to postpone, de-prioritize, or kill the IG program. Focusing efforts on clearly established business objectives will largely ameliorate this inherent problem of conflicting agendas.

Sometimes all an unenthusiastic executive sponsor has to do is wait for the natural inertia of the over-sized and lethargic IG steering committee to weight things down, and soon other projects and programs that are more routine and cost-justifiable in the short-term take resources from the IG effort. It then may fade into the background until there is a new litigation disaster, major compliance failure, massive security breach or other such IG drivers.

There is a way to make these IG planning teams more effective, agile, and accountable: *tiering your IG steering committee* and staggering meeting requirements to bring in only those needed while not wasting everyone else's time.

Otherwise, the IG program initiative will follow the same predictable and sluggish cycle it did before, only with a slightly different set of players.

How would an organization approach structuring their IG steering committee for better results? Here are some guidelines:

1. **Have a clear executive sponsor**- the IG lead for organization we have worked with proclaimed, "We don't have to worry about an executive sponsor - we have four of them!" This sounds like good news at first, but when you consider the varying and conflicting agendas of the four executive sponsors it becomes rather obvious that this is less than the ideal scenario. A clear leader who has authority can help focus IG efforts and deliver results in the form of early wins to keep feeding and growing the IG program. The executive sponsor should be apprised of

progress and should sign off on milestones and major policy decisions as they are presented to them by a small subset of leaders from the IG steering committee;

2. **Form a high-level 'decision committee';** - this can be a group of three, four, or at the most, five leaders from the functional areas most involved in your IG efforts. They are the ones who are to be held accountable for delivering results and keeping the IG program on track. They should meet regularly, probably weekly, to drive the IG program forward. Their focus should be on focus, that is, focusing the efforts of the IG steering committee and delegating specific tasks to ensure tangible results are delivered from small early wins and the IG program expands in a logical way that focuses on meeting business objectives;

3. **Form subject matter expert (SME) teams** - using cross-functional team members. In a sort of matrix organizational structure, create teams to center effort on key areas of IG impact, and to cross-train each other. For instance, your e-discovery readiness team should include members from legal staff, but also (depending on your specific scenario) records management, IT, and perhaps the business unit that is most involved or embroiled in litigation. Your data governance (DG) SME team must include your DG lead, but also members from privacy, security, IT and key business units. Recommendations from the SME teams should be made to the decision committee for final deliberation, and then presented to the executive sponsor for sign-off and approval (or rejection to re-work the approach);

4. **Keep all members of the IG steering committee updated**- keep them in the loop with frequent updates on progress and decisions. Don't waste their time with a meeting when an email or update to your intranet or collaborative site will do;

5. **Convene the entire IG steering group only when necessary**- perhaps every two weeks in the initial phases of your IG program but at least monthly. Have a standing meeting that does not conflict with IG steering committee members' schedules to the extent possible.

Additional tips: for those who cannot attend a formal IG program meeting, make sure they are tuned in via video conference or at least via conference call. Do not allow excuses for non-participation. And make sure you tie the tasks and progress of the IG program effort directly to stated business objectives.

Stay focused and do not waste IG steering committee members' time. Lay out a meeting schedule that makes sense and structure the IG team into more agile, accountable units which can meet on their own and not waste others' time.

The Emerging Role of the CIGO

A key challenge is that because of the inter-disciplinary requirements for implementing IG—no one wants to *own* IG. It touches on parts of the strengths of a CIO or General Counsel or Information Security Manager or Chief Compliance Officer, but it also requires them to go out of their comfort zone into new areas.

According to research, the two most common IG executive sponsors are General Counsel and CIOs. Sometimes IG programs are led by an organization's General Counsel, and they may be well-versed in privacy law, but they may not have the technology chops to understand exactly how to apply complex new IG-enabling technologies, and they may understand retention schedules but are not up to speed on records management best practices. Sometimes IG programs are led by the CIO, who may be well-versed in security and aware of privacy issues, but often CIOs and records managers don't speak the same language: a "record" means something totally different to a CIO than to a records manager; also, legal research isn't the CIO's job and the general counsel will always have to make those decisions anyway.

So whose baby is IG?

There is a need for a new job title to pull all these disciplines together into a cohesive IG program: Chief Information Governance Officer (CIGO).

The CIGO will have to be a top-flight executive who understands and is near-expert not only in IT, but also legal and compliance issues, records management issues, privacy issues, security tools and techniques and business issues. They must also have outstanding communications and management skills. That's a tough bill to fill.

A CIGO can act in a coordinating function, but lacking authority, their efforts will likely be met with resistance. Because of its requirements, the CIGO should perhaps have authority over the CIO, chief information security officer (CISO), and chief privacy officer (CPO), and even CFO. The CIGO is very nearly a chief operations officer (COO), and that should probably be whom the CIGO reports to, if not the EVP of Risk, or even the CEO. It is a crucial job that mostly is not being filled. However, there is a great need for it, and it can demonstrate tangible results.

CHAPTER SUMMARY: **KEY POINTS**

- **Implementing IG programs requires a cross-functional approach.**
- IG programs require a strong executive sponsor.
- The top tier of an IG steering committee should include: Legal, IT, Records Management, Info Security, Privacy.
- Tiering your IG steering committee keeps it more agile and able to make decisions.
- Due to the inter-disciplinary requirements for implementing IG—no one wants to *own* IG.
- Chief IG Officer (CIGO) is a new title for a person heading up IG programs.
- The CIGO must be proficient in legal issues, infosec, records management privacy and more.

Robert Smallwood

Chapter 4

How Do You Implement Information Governance?

IG has a lot of moving parts, so it requires that you set up an **IG framework**, which provides the guardrails to guide your decisions.

An IG framework includes: 1) your business objectives; 2) your executive sponsor; 3) IG steering committee; 4) IG lead; 5) relevant standards and best practices; 6) an evaluation of external and internal business considerations; 7) IG reference models or frameworks; 8) program metrics and auditing; and, 9) your communications and training plan. The IG framework you build should be customized for your business needs. We will go into more detail on these components in this chapter.

You may notice throughout this book that we emphasize one key fact repeatedly: Securing a sponsor at the executive management level is critical—it is the *most important factor for IG success.*

Executive sponsorship is a key IG best practice. Program failure is a great risk without an executive sponsor. Such a program likely will fade or fizzle out or be relegated to the back burner. Without strong high-level leadership, when things go awry, finger pointing and political games may take over, impeding progress and cooperation.

An executive must be on board and supporting the effort in order to garner the resources needed to develop and execute the strategic IG plan, and that executive must be held accountable for the development and execution of the plan. These axioms apply to developing and carrying out an IG strategic plan.

Also, resources are needed—time, human capital, budget money, new technologies. The first is a critical element: It is not possible to require managers to take time out of their other duties to participate in a project if there is no executive edict and consistent follow up, support, and communication. Perhaps you should update performance review metrics to include a component that measures IG policy conformance.

The executive sponsor serves six key purposes in a program:

1. **Budget.** The executive sponsor ensures an adequate financial commitment is made to see that project milestones are met as part of the program and lobbies for additional expenditures when change orders are made or cost overruns occur.

2. **Planning and control.** The executive sponsor sets direction and tracks accomplishment of specific, measurable business objectives.

3. **Decision making.** The executive sponsor makes or approves crucial decisions and resolves issues that are escalated for resolution.

4. **Expectation Management.** The executive sponsor must manage expectation, since success is quite often a stakeholder perception.

5. **Anticipation.** Every project that is competing for resources can run into unforeseen blockages and objections. Executive sponsors run interference and provide political might for the PM to lead the project to completion, through a series of milestones.

6. **Approvals.** The executive sponsor signs off when milestones and objectives have been met.

The higher your executive sponsor is in the organization, the better.[ii] The implementation of an IG program may be driven by the General Counsel, chief information officer (CIO), chief risk officer, or, ideally, as the Sedona Conference and IG Initiative have recommended, a Chief IG Officer (CIGO). The CIGO must have the mandate and authority to drive the program forward.

If the sponsor is the chief executive officer (CEO), so much the better. With CEO sponsorship come many of the key elements needed to complete a successful project, including allocated management time, management priority, and budget money.

Crucial Executive Sponsor Role

The role of an executive sponsor is high level, requiring periodic and regular attention to the status of the program, particularly with budget issues, staff resources, and milestone progress. The role of a project or **program manager** (PM) is more detailed and day-to-day, tracking specific tasks that must be executed to make progress toward milestones. Both roles are essential. The savvy PM brings in the executive sponsor to push things along when more authority is needed but reserves such program capital for those issues that absolutely cannot be resolved without executive intervention. It is best for the PM to keep the executive sponsor fully informed but to ask for assistance only when absolutely needed.

At the same time, the PM must manage the relationship with the executive sponsor, perhaps with some gentle reminders, coaxing, or prodding, to ensure that the role and tasks of executive sponsorship are being fulfilled. "[T]he successful Project Manager knows that if those duties are not being fulfilled, it's time to call a timeout and have a serious conversation with the Executive Sponsor about the viability of the project."[iii]

An eager and effective executive sponsor makes all the difference to a program—if the role is properly managed by the PM. It is a tricky relationship, since the PM is always below the executive sponsor in the organization's hierarchy, yet the PM must coax the superior into tackling certain high-level tasks. Sometimes a third-party consultant who is an expert in the specific project can instigate and support requests made of the sponsor and provide a solid business rationale.

While the executive sponsor role is high level, the PM's role and tasks are more detailed and involve day-to-day management.

Evolving Role of the Executive Sponsor

The role of the executive sponsor necessarily evolves and changes over the life of the initial IG program launch, during the implementation phases, and on through the continued IG program.

To get the program off the ground, the executive sponsor must first own the business case. They must make a solid business case and get adequate budgetary funding and resources.

Some cost savings as a result of direct actions within the IG program can add to the cost/benefit analysis. But an IG effort takes more than money; it takes *time*—not just time to develop new policies, redesign processes, and implement new technologies, but the time of the designated PM, program leaders, and needed program team members.

In order to get this time set aside, the IG program must be made a top priority of the organization. It must be recognized, formalized, and aligned with organizational objectives. All this up-front work is the responsibility of the executive sponsor.

Once the IG steering committee is formed, team members must clearly understand why the new program is important and how it will help the organization meet its business objectives. This message must be regularly reinforced by the executive sponsor; he or she must not only paint the vision of the future state of the organization but articulate the steps in the path to get there.

When the formal program effort commences, the executive sponsor must remain visible and accessible. They cannot disappear into everyday duties and expect the program team to carry the effort through. The executive sponsor must be there to help the team confront and overcome business obstacles as they arise and must praise the successes along the way. This requires active involvement and a willingness to spend the time to keep the program on track and focused.

The executive sponsor must be the lighthouse that shows the way even through cloudy skies and rough waters. This person is the captain who must steer the ship, even if the first mate (PM) is seasick and the deckhands (program team) are drenched and tired.

After the program is implemented, the executive sponsor is responsible for maintaining its effectiveness and relevance. This is done through periodic compliance audits, testing and sampling, and scheduled meetings with the ongoing PM.

*   *   *   *   *

Building Your IG Framework

Once your executive sponsor is in place, you must build an **information governance framework** (IGF) which is the foundation of your IG program. Without it, you will end up with a weak and unstable program that will likely fail, as many have.

Each IG framework will look a little different but there are commonalities that appear in successful ones. An IGF needs to be modified according to the terrain (competitive industry scenario) and elements (external business environment) and available labor and building materials (internal human resources, skillsets, and budget).

Here are the key components of an IG Framework that will serve as the construct, the foundation for your successful IG program:

- **Business Objectives** - This is where you start. Your organizational goals and objectives are the key reason for implementing an IG program. They provide the business rationale for investing resources. The objectives for the IG program must align with and support the organization's overall strategic plan and IT strategy.

- **Executive Sponsor** - The person with the money and the motivation to build the IG program. The executive sponsor is involved with developing the blueprint and overall building plan but leaves the specifics to those with expertise in key areas. He or she stays in the loop, and, at times, may have to intervene. However also, other times, the executive sponsor is the one offering coffee and donuts in the morning, or springing for a pizza party on a Friday afternoon after a long week of work where good progress was made. A good executive sponsor uses both carrots and sticks.

- **IG Lead** - This person is accountable for executing the IG strategic plan and completing milestones within the budget, resource, and time constraints approved by the executive sponsor. The IG lead could be the organization's General Counsel, CIO, Chief Risk Officer, even CEO, or ideally, as the Sedona Conference and IG Initiative have called for, the Chief IG Officer.

- **Cross-functional IG Team** - Just as architects, bricklayers, plumbers, electricians and carpenters are needed to build a house, an IG program will need a blend of professionals. They should be leaders in key functional areas, including: legal, IT, privacy, security, records management, and also business unit heads/information owners, and potentially other key areas such as change management, risk management, communications, training, and other specialties as appropriate. Your IG team will have a different makeup from your neighbor's IG team, as business objectives, resources, corporate culture and other variables are different, even if you are in the same industry.

- **Survey and Evaluate External Factors** - Once you have an IG team in place and the IG plan is harmonized and aligned with your organization's strategic plan and IT strategy, you have made fair progress. .

- **Program Communications & Training** - Your IG program must include a communications and training component as a standard function. Your stakeholder audience must be made aware of new policies and practices that are to be followed, and how this new approach contributes toward accomplishing business objectives. But critically, they must receive training on the new approach, and constant and consistent reinforcement of new IG precepts.

- **Program Metrics, Monitoring, Auditing & Enforcement** - How do you know how well you are doing? An IG program must have established metrics and controls to determine the level of employee compliance, its impact on key operational areas, and progress made toward key business objectives. Testing and auditing provide an opportunity to give feedback to employees on how well they are doing and to recommend changes they may make. In addition, having objective feedback on key metrics also will allow your executive sponsor to see where progress has been made, and where improvements need to focus.

By including the above elements in your IG framework your organization will have established a solid foundation to build your IG program, and it will have greatly increased its odds of success.

IG Requires Change Management

It is important to bear in mind that an IG effort is truly a change management effort, in that it aims to change the structure, guidelines, and rules within which employees operate. The change must occur at the very core of the organization's culture. It must be embedded permanently, and for it to be, the message must be constantly and consistently reinforced. Achieving this kind of change requires commitment from the very highest levels of the organization.

Which Technologies Help to Enable IG Programs and Enforce Controls?

We are going to do a brief overview of the key information technologies that help enable and monitor information-related processes. Let's start with that short definition of IG and go through them.

IG, in short, is defined as "security, control, & optimization of information." That covers a lot of ground. Let's look at some categories of products that may be leveraged in your IG program. This is not an exhaustive list but rather a demonstrative one.

Let's start with "Security" of information:

1) Electronic document security - technologies in this group include information rights management (IRM), and its little brother, file encryption. IRM technology secures confidential e-documents by controlling the "rights" to view, print, edit, forward, copy, or save e-documents. The rights can even be controlled by time of day (e.g. access during work hours only) or type of device (e.g. access on your PC but not mobile devices). Rights are assigned upon creation of the document, usually according to roles (levels) in the organization. These access rights travel with the e-document itself, and access can be turned off remotely (via the Cloud) if an employee has had their laptop or computing device compromised or stolen, or if the employee has been terminated. So even if Sony Pictures was hacked and completely compromised, confidential documents would still be protected, in an encrypted state. Or if an Edward Snowden accesses hundreds of thousands of files, they would not be viewable and could not be copied or printed. Certainly, technologies in this category are a part of supporting an IG program;

2) Data loss prevention (DLP) - software that continuously monitors and thoroughly inspects information that flows (e.g. email, e-documents) on a network and does not allow sensitive information containing certain key words or phrases to exit the firewall. DLP protects information in all three states: 1) At rest; 2) In use; and 3) In transit. Often used in conjunction with IRM software and also to assist in data mapping efforts;

3) Digital signatures - carry detailed audit information used to detect unauthorized modifications to e-documents and to authenticate the identity of the signatory;

4) Database activity monitoring (DAM) - and database auditing tools monitor databases in real time for anomalies and unusual activity, and create an audit trail generated in real time that can be the forensic smoking gun when attacks have occurred;

5) Print security - to help secure large print files—which contain highly useful information for hackers as the information is distilled and in one place—specialized hardware devices designed to sit between the print server and the network "cloak" print files and they are only visible to those who have a properly configured cloaking device on the other end;

6) Security vulnerability/penetration testing software - software in this category allows organizations to test and find any security vulnerabilities they may have, and to address these weaknesses through security patches and other methods;

7) Stream messaging- for confidential communications, this approach leaves no record of an email exchange, that is, once the email message is read, it "vaporizes" completely. This prevents printing, forwarding or altering the message.

Now let's move to "Control" of information:

1) Identity and Access Management (IAM)- controls logon credentials, and aims to prevent unauthorized access. IAM governs access to information through an automated, continuous process. Implemented properly, IAM keeps access limited to authorized users;

2) Document analytics- this type of software monitors access, use, and printing of e-documents in real time. Graphical reports are created—so if a user normally downloads or prints 100 documents a day, and on one day they download or print 1,000 or 10,000—red flags go off;

3) Document labeling- is the process of attaching a label to classify a document, which is a simple way to increase user awareness about the sensitivity of a document, for instance, by labeling it "confidential;"

4) Business Process Management Suites (BPMS)- this software allows organizations to control business processes and to model and simulate business process routing and processing options to automate a process from end to end. The ability to make intelligent changes in process based on metrics and real-time feedback facilitates optimization of the efficiency of business processes.

5) Enterprise Content Management (ECM) – to manage all types of unstructured content. ECM controls access and manages versions of e-documents, web pages, reports and other digital assets. ECM is being somewhat displaced by cloud-based **Enterprise File Synch and Share (EFSS)** platforms such as Box.

6) Mobile Device Management (MDM)- to manage and control your network of mobile devices. MDM allows an organization to update mobile devices en masse with security patches and updates, to remotely wipe lost or stolen devices of confidential data, and to monitor the mobile network.[10]

Now let's look at "Optimization" of information:

1) Predictive coding- during the early case assessment (ECA) phase of e-discovery, predictive coding is a "court endorsed process" that can be utilized for document review. Legal experts review a subset of documents and "teach" the software which documents are responsive in a particular legal matter, and the software goes through a sorting and sifting process to find similar documents. This is an iterative process where the human legal expert continues to review a sampling of the documents found by the software to provide input and facilitate improved accuracy by the software in finding responsive documents. The result is *drastically reduced costs for document review*, which can be accomplished in a much shorter timeframe giving legal teams more insights and more time to develop strategy. Predictive analytics can also help you to find new insights and trends to act

61

upon, perhaps to improve operational efficiency, cross-sell customers, or even to develop new products and services;

2) Business intelligence (BI) - uses software tools and techniques to analyze raw (structured) data to help provide useful insights for managers and executives to make more informed decisions. New insights into the data can be gleaned which can help spur innovation in marketing, product development, finance, and other key business areas;

3) Content analytics (CA)- Content analytics software applies BI and business analytics to better gain insights into content volumes and patterns, and how the content may be used. CA can help improve findability of websites, brands, and products;

4) Master data management (MDM)- this type of software helps organizations to perform data governance and data quality functions, which are key to IG efforts not only in the IT department but also in business units. The goal of MDM software is to ensure that accurate, reliable data from a single source is leveraged across business units. That is, the key aim is to establish, "a single version of the truth" and eliminate multiple, inconsistent versions of data sets. Downstream reports which rely on this data are therefore more accurate and trusted by managers;

5) File analysis, classification, and remediation (FACR) - software tools in this category scan your entire collection of information (e.g. e-documents) - across shared drives, storage area networks, and all other storage devices to conduct "file analysis" that is, determining the author, topic, file type, date of creation, date of last access, etc. This process can help an organization locate where personal confidential information like PII, PHI and PCI is stored so they may protect it with encryption, and also to dispose of it as is legally required. Further, the more sophisticated tools can actually begin to insert classification metadata tags to help organize the content and to assist in the remediation process, which includes deleting duplicates and "data debris" which no longer has business value to the organization.

So, with just the above examples, you can see *quite clearly* that there are a number of tools you can leverage to address various aspects of your IG program.

CHAPTER SUMMARY: **KEY POINTS**

- **An IG framework provides the guardrails to guide decisions in your IG program.**
- A strong executive sponsor is critical to IG program success.
- Begin your IG planning with a focus on organizational business objectives.
- IG requires a *change management* effort.
- There are a number of key technologies that help to secure, control and optimize information.

Chapter 5

Where Do You Start with an Information Governance Program?

7 Key IG Accelerators to Launch Your Program

One of biggest problems with kicking off new IG programs is that they take on average a year or more to form, according to industry research. Beyond that, many IG programs lose steam and fail to meet the organization's objectives. This can occur for a variety of reasons, adhering to the Anna Karenina principle, which derives from the opening to Tolstoy's book,

> "Happy families are all alike; every unhappy family
> is unhappy in its own way."

That is to say every IG program failure is unique and due to a mix of shortcomings.

One IG industry leader confided, "I have designed perfect IG programs and nothing happened." In this case, there likely were significant weaknesses in the approach, including lack of strong executive sponsorship and developing a clear business case.

Other failed IG programs may not have had the right mix of players named to the IG Steering Committee. Others may not have properly planned roles and a clear RACI matrix (which identifies those Responsible, Accountable, Consulted, and Informed) early on which doomed the program to failure. Still others may have lost focus on the organizational change management and communications aspects which are required to keep an IG program on track.

But there have been some lessons learned from these failures, and the approaches to creating and maintaining successful IG programs are starting to coalesce. Here are seven key accelerators which can help launch or expand your IG program:

1) Recruit a strong executive sponsor- As noted in the previous chapter and in other sections of this book, not enough can be said about recruiting a strong executive sponsor. If there are multiple executive sponsors on board then nominate the most senior one, or if that is not logical, the one with the most commitment (and the most to lose or gain). If you have none and are evaluating executive sponsors, find that person who has the highest information risk levels, the one who has the most to lose from a data breach, from noncompliance fines, or from soaring legal costs. Or even rapidly increasing information storage costs. Think General Counsel, CIO, COO, Chief Risk Officer, Chief Information Security Officer, Chief Privacy Officer, and similar titles. (Ideally, the CEO is a solid choice). They have clear budget and decision authority. These senior executives likely have been considering various piecemeal measures and you can educate them on the benefits of taking a holistic IG approach and aligning the effort with strategic business objectives.[11]

2) Find common ground - most larger organizations have some form of a data governance or at least data quality program on an ongoing basis. The goals of a data governance program align with higher level IG program goals. Remember, IG programs must be driven from the top down, but implemented from the bottom up for best results. So this should be a good marriage. Find your natural allies. If your organization is planning to implement real-time email archiving, and your email policy is going to have to be reviewed and revised, this is a good time to dovetail off that project to launch a fledgling IG effort. If you are in records management, your skills can be helpful in working with your General Counsel to improve litigation readiness, reduce legal e-discovery costs, and reduce attorney document review costs. If you are in IT you may want to team with the records management lead and approach business unit leaders who have the biggest information management problems or the most litigation and help them improve their approach to records and e-document management;

3) Leverage Audit Findings - an internal audit of procedures and practices may reveal weaknesses that are putting your information at risk. If you are looking to gain a mandate for IG, findings from an internal audit can provide the mandate for moving forward with an IG program;[12]

4) Piggyback on existing IT projects - especially those that are approved and funded, or those that are likely to. For instance, if your organization is due for a refresh in enterprise content management (ECM) software, or you are cleaning up shared drives and/or migrating to SharePoint, this would be an ideal time to go a step further and implement a more comprehensive IG program that can work in lockstep with the ECM implementation. If you have a Chief Data Officer and robust data governance program, IG is a natural fit. If legal hold notification (LHN) has been implemented and now additional efficiencies in the e-discovery process are being pursued, a broader IG approach may be well-timed;[13]

5) Emphasize hard cost savings- show a hard dollar benefit, and then layer on the benefits of information risk reduction, reputational risk reduction, improved compliance capabilities, improved productivity, and improved efficiency in implementing legal holds and other litigation-related tasks. Where do you find those hard dollar savings? An easy target is storage. With a current and complete data map and leveraging file analysis tools you can show executives which information is worthless redundant, outdated or trivial (ROT) and how much storage costs can be cut or at least the rate of growth can be slowed. Other cost impact areas may be reductions in cyber-insurance costs and e-discovery costs due to an ongoing IG program;[14]

6) Cite the impact of poor IG - one large financial institution we worked with presented their executives with a list of all the compliance fines that their competitors have paid—sometimes into the billions—when making the case for moving forward with an IG program. You may also want to cite "worst case" general examples of breaches of PII that have heavily damaged companies like Sony Pictures, Anthem, and Target;[15]

7) Establishing a legal defense - if executives still are not convinced, then let them know that in cases like Sony Pictures and Anthem, where employees or customers have had their personal data compromised, there will be lawsuits. And if an organization has an IG program in place and has taken reasonable "best effort" steps to secure sensitive information including PII and protected health information (PHI), then the foundation for a legal defense is in place, and although culpability may be found, the awards will be smaller which lowers the cost of legal claims.[16]

These are just some of the accelerators that can help get your IG program launched or expanded.

CHAPTER SUMMARY: **KEY POINTS**

- **IG programs must be driven from the top down, and implemented from the bottom up.**
- IG programs fail for a variety of reasons.
- A strong executive sponsor is crucial.
- Find your natural internal allies to launch an IG effort—those who have the most to gain from IG.
- Findings from an internal audit can provide the mandate for moving forward with an IG program.
- Piggyback on existing, funded IT projects such as a move to a new enterprise content management (ECM) system to help launch your IG program.
- Show hard dollar savings, and then add the benefits of info risk reduction to justify IG.
- Cite the "worst case" impact of poor IG when making your business case to move forward.
- An IG program in place means your management has taken reasonable "best effort" steps to secure confidential information and PII, which can help a future legal defense.

Chapter 6

Building the Business Case

The best way to measure the viability of an IG program is by determining if the investment of time and resources is going to be a profitable one. Beyond that, the benefits of information and legal risk reduction must be made clear.

The executive sponsor must develop and *own* the business case, so it is important to get it right. You must look for hard dollar savings where possible, establish meaningful metrics, and attempt to quantify the value of information risk reduction.

There are clear tangible and intangible benefits to implementing IG, but fears of compliance violations and major fines, spiraling e-discovery costs, theft of intellectual property (IP), leakage of personally identifiable information (PII), or even the prospect of criminal charges may be sufficient to justify the IG program.

Legally defensible deletion of information is going to be a key driver of cost reduction in your IG program. Getting rid of all that redundant, outdated, and trivial (ROT) information—which may be 40%-70% of what your organization manages—will drive down hard storage costs, reduce legal and compliance risks, and make information more findable and accessible for knowledge workers, boosting their productivity while improving the professional work environment.

"The sheer volume of information, combined with the speed of its accumulation (velocity) and the lack of effective management is at the root of the problem. This surplus of electronically stored information (ESI) is, in reality, driving up the cost of storage, raising the cost and risk of eDiscovery and regulatory compliance, negatively impacting employee productivity, and raising the prospect of intellectual property theft and PII leakage."[17]

Your IG program addresses all these growing challenges.

Critical questions to raise during the decision-making process include: What if we are not able to meet legal demands for records production during litigation? What can happen if auditors or regulators investigated our recordkeeping practices? These types of serious questions must be asked and can only be addressed with a successful IG program.

One Big Negative Event Can Change the Ballgame

Just as the September 11th attacks and Hurricane Katrina changed the realities of disaster recovery and business continuity plans, and the WikiLeaks scandal changed the realities of e-document security, one large adverse event—a major data breach or particularly costly lawsuit—can change the way your organization thinks about managing information.

The first step in launching an IG program is to understand what key factors qualify a project as viable in a particular organization. Once that is known, steps to build the business case that satisfy or exceed those requirements can be taken.

According to Osterman Research, in its report entitled, *The True ROI of Information Governance*, the top three drivers for justifying and IG program are:

1) Risk avoidance;

2) Regulatory risk mitigation; and,

3) Employee productivity improvement.[18]

As noted in that report, having a comprehensive understanding of your total costs before and after applying any solutions is the key to building a believable ROI Model. The costs you might focus on in your target area maybe be as simple as information storage costs, or more complex and somewhat of a moving target like e-discovery collection and review costs. (Often it is tough to get your legal team to break these out accurately).

Once you have the baseline costs determined, estimated savings can be calculated using whatever financial model suits your organization.

Hard Cost Savings

1. **Information Collection During Litigation:** As the volume and velocity of electronically stored information (ESI) rises, so will eDiscovery costs during litigation rise, and the costs and effort to classify, categorize and manage ESI on a daily basis. End users will take the path of least resistance, which means the information will be organized in accordance the skillset of those end users, and with a minimum of effort. The lack of consistency will ultimately add to information collection costs whenever there is an eDiscovery request.[19]

2. **Document Review for Litigation**: this function is usually done by attorneys or high-end paralegals at an hourly billing rate per document, or per megabyte. The more documents subject to legal review, the higher the cost. By proactively removing unnecessary and irrelevant ESI, fewer documents will have to be reviewed, resulting in lowering review costs.

3. **Information Storage Savings:** Contrary to what many believe about storage costs getting cheaper, the exact opposite is true for organizations today, (which rely on online access to enterprise storage), due to rapidly increasing volumes. One must consider the full cost of information ownership, which includes not only storage hardware but floor space, air conditioning, electricity to run the hardware and software, maintenance and support costs, staff salaries, contractor costs, and physical and software security to name a few. As

noted in the Osterman report, "an IG program will deliver two areas of storage savings: the percentage of storage resources freed up due to more efficient and ongoing data retention/disposition procedures, and the continuing storage savings from an ongoing defensible disposition practice."[20]

Soft Costs – Intangible Cost Offsets

1. **Potential Revenue Gains:** Often overlooked is the gain in revenue as a result of recovered employee productivity. When employees spend fewer hours searching and/or re-creating information, they spend more time engaged in activities that will generate more revenue for the organization. That enhanced productivity can generate real top line revenue growth. [21] In addition, performing analytics on cleaned data will provide new insights that may result in new revenue-generating product and service innovations.

2. **Information Risk Reduction:** Risk avoidance involves taking steps to mitigate exposure to negative events. Risk mitigation is a key component and goal of IG programs. Your risk may take the form of improving the odds of winning lawsuits due to efficient collection and review of responsive information, giving your legal team more time and resources to spend on strategy. At the same time your organization will be lowering its risk of court sanctions and fines, which can be substantial and turn into the millions. Further, you are guarding against breaches and protecting your brand while reducing your exposure to reputational risk.[22]

3. **Improvements in Knowledge Worker Productivity:** When your highest-paid professionals cannot locate information to make a decision, they waste time searching and may ultimately end up doing double-work by re-creating the information. This is difficult to calculate but it is a real cost. An average knowledge worker can spend 15%-25% of their workweek simply *searching* for information. You want to shoot for providing the

right information to the right people at the right time—securely. When this is the aim of your IG program, substantial productivity benefits will accrue and you will be promoting a more professional and efficient work environment, while minimizing your staffing needs.

CHAPTER SUMMARY: **KEY POINTS**

- **The executive sponsor must develop and *own* the business case.**
- Legally defensible deletion of information is going to be a key driver of cost reduction in your IG program.
- One major data breach or costly lawsuit can provide the justification for an IG program.
- Major hard dollar savings come from E-discovery collection and document review cost reductions.
- Information storage costs can be significantly reduced with IG.
- You may find opportunities for revenue growth by analyzing data in your IG program effort.
- Risk mitigation is a key component and goal of IG programs.
- Substantial productivity benefits will accrue from cleaner, more accessible information due to IG.

Chapter 7

Overseeing the IG Program

Maintaining your IG program beyond an initial project effort is key to realizing continued and long-term benefits of IG. This means that the IG program must be "evergreen" and become an everyday part of an organization's operations and communications. There is continuing work to do after an initial IG program push.

Program Communications and Training

Your IG program must contain a communications and training component, as a standard function. Your stakeholder audience must be made aware of the new policies and practices that are to be followed, and how this new approach contributes toward the organization's goals and business objectives.

The first step in your communications plan is to identify and segment your stakeholder audiences, and to customize or modify your message to the degree that is necessary to be effective. Communications to your IT team can have a more technical slant, and communications to your legal team can have some legal jargon and emphasize legal issues. The more forethought you put into crafting your communications strategy the more effective it will be.

That is not to say that *all* messages must have several versions: there are some core concepts and goals that should be emphasized in communications to all employees.

Training should take multiple avenues as well. Some can be classroom instruction, some online learning, and you may want to create a series of training videos. But the training effort must be consistent and ongoing to maintain high levels of IG effectiveness. Certainly, this means you will need a special addition to your new hire training program for employees joining or transferring to your organization.

Program Controls, Monitoring, Auditing and Enforcement

How do you know how well you are doing? You will need to develop metrics to determine the level of employee compliance, its impact on key operational areas, and progress made toward established business objectives.

Testing and auditing the program provides an opportunity to give feedback to employees on how well they are doing, and to recommend changes they may make. But also, having objective feedback on key metrics will allow your executive sponsor to see where progress has been made, and also, where improvements need to focus.

Clear penalties for policy violations must be communicated to employees so they know the seriousness of the IG program, and how important it is in helping the organization pursue its business goals and accomplish stated business objectives.

Similar to a workplace safety program, ongoing training and communications are important, to keep employees apprised of approved processes and behaviors which support IG. Also important is regular feedback based on established metrics to see how you are doing.

This requires vigilant and consistent monitoring and auditing to ensure that IG policies and processes are effective and consistently followed and enforced. If proper controls are in place this should become a regular part of the enterprise's operations.

Monitoring and Accountability

This requires a continuous tightening down and expansion of protections and the implementation of newer, strategic technologies. Information technology (IT) developments and innovations that can foster the effort must be steadily monitored and evaluated, and those technology subsets that can assist in providing security need to be incorporated into the mix.

The IG policies themselves—for email, handling of confidential information, use of social media, cloud use and so forth—must be reviewed and updated periodically to accommodate changes in the business environment, laws, regulations, and technology. Program gaps and failures must be addressed and the effort should continue to improve and adapt to new types of security threats.

That means accountability. Maintaining an IG program requires that someone is accountable for continually monitoring and refinement of policies and tools. Some individual must remain responsible for an IG policy's administration and results.[23]

Perhaps the executive sponsor for the initial project becomes the chief information governance officer (CIGO) or IG "Czar" of sorts; or the chief executive officer (CEO) continues ownership of the program and drives its active improvement. The organization may also decide to form a standing IG board, steering committee, or team with specific responsibilities for monitoring, maintaining, and advancing the program.

However it takes shape, an IG program must be ongoing, dynamic, and aggressive in its execution in order to remain effective.

Staffing Continuity Plan

In today's work environment, turnover is more frequent than in the past. People leave to take new career opportunities outside of the organization, and also change jobs and move to other positions within an organization, so it is critical to have a staffing continuity plan for your IG program. Backup and supporting designates must be named, and kept current on the administration of the program. So, you may have a "supporting sponsor" or "senior sponsor" to fill the role of executive sponsor, should the need arise; and likewise there needs to be other human resource/staffing redundancies built in to assure the smooth and continued operation of the IG program, in the event of an unplanned incident that threatens it.

This may mean that when the formal program manager is unable to be there to execute their duties, an assistant or designated backup can carry out those duties.

It is also a good idea to cross-train employees. With this approach, the legal team, for instance, will better understand the needs and requirements of the records management function, and vice-versa. IT will better understand Legal's needs. Records management will better understand Legal, and so forth. Cross-training improves overall organization acceptance and understanding of the IG program, while building in safeguards to ensure it keeps running.

Continuous Process Improvement

Maintaining IG program effectives requires implementing principles of continuous process improvement (CPI). CPI is a "never-ending effort to discover and eliminate the main causes of problems." It accomplishes this by using small-steps improvements, rather than implementing one huge improvement. In Japan, the word kaizen reflects this gradual and constant process, as it is enacted throughout the organization, regardless of department, position, or level.[24] To remain effective, the program must continue using CPI methods and techniques.

Maintaining and improving the program will require monitoring tools, periodic audits, and regular meetings for discussion and approval of changes to improve the program. It will require a cross-section of team leaders from IT, legal, records management, compliance, internal audit, and risk management, and also functional business units participating actively and citing possible threats and sources of information leakage.

Why Continuous Improvement is Needed

While the specific drivers of change are always evolving, the reasons that organizations need to continuously improve their program for securing information assets are relatively constant, and include:

- **Changing Technology**. New technology capabilities need to be monitored and considered with an eye to improving, streamlining, or reducing the cost of IG. The IG program needs to anticipate new types of threats and also evaluate adding or replacing technologies to continue to improve it.

- **Changing Laws and Regulations**. Compliance with new or updated laws and regulations must be maintained.

- **Internal Information Governance Requirements**. As an organization updates and improves its overall IG, the program elements that concern critical information assets must be kept aligned and synchronized.

- **Changing Business Plans**. As the enterprise develops new business strategies and enters new markets, it must reconsider and update its IG program. If, for instance, a firm moves from being a domestic entity to a regional or global one, new laws and regulations will apply, and perhaps new

81

threats will exist and new security strategies must be formed.

- **Evolving Industry Best Practices**. Best practices change and new best practices arise with the introduction of each successive wave of technology, and with changes in the business environment. The program should consider and leverage new best practices.

- **Fixing Program Shortcomings**. Addressing flaws in the IG program that are discovered through testing, monitoring, and auditing; or addressing an actual breach of confidential information; or a legal sanction imposed due to noncompliance are all reasons why a program must be revisited periodically and kept updated.[25]

Maintaining the IG program requires that a senior level officer of the enterprise continues to sponsor it and pushes for enforcement, improvement, and expansion. This requires leadership, and consistent and clear messages to employees. IG and the security of information assets must be on the minds of all members of the enterprise; it must be something they are aware of and think about daily. They must be on the lookout for ways to improve it, and they should be rewarded for those contributions.

Gaining this level of mindshare in employees' heads will require follow up messages in the form of personal speeches and presentations, newsletters, corporate announcements, e-mail messages, and even posters placed at strategic points (e.g., near the shared printing station advising about secure procedures). Everyone must be reminded that keeping information assets secure is everyone's job, and that to lose, misuse or leak confidential information harms the organization over the long term and erodes its value.

CHAPTER SUMMARY: **KEY POINTS**

- **Lines of authority, accountability, & responsibility must be clear for the IG program to succeed long-term.**
- IG program communications should be consistent and clear, and customized for various stakeholder groups.
- IG program audits are an opportunity to improve training & compliance, not to punish employees.
- An effective IG program requires vigilant and consistent monitoring and auditing to ensure that IG policies are followed and enforced.
- Information technologies that can assist in advancing the program must be steadily monitored, evaluated, and implemented.
- **To maintain and improve the IG program will require monitoring tools, regular audits, and regular meetings for discussion and approval of changes to the program to continually improve it.**
- IG programs need built-in staffing redundancies to ensure their continued operation in the event of employee turnover or transfer.
- Organizations need to continuously improve their program for securing information assets
- Maintaining an IG program requires that an executive sponsor continues to push for enforcement, improvement, and expansion of the program to secure and control information.

Robert Smallwood

Part 2

IG Planning & Policy Development

Chapter 8

Information Governance Principles

A Blueprint for IG Success

Using guiding principles to drive your IG program can help focus efforts and maintain consistency.

The following 10 IG Principles are the result of synthesizing, analyzing, and distilling a great deal of information on IG program successes, failures, and Best Practices. These IG principles are a good starting point toward someday establishing "Generally Accepted IG Principles."

Here are 10 IG principles that must be addressed and adhered to for IG programs to succeed:

1) Stakeholder consultation. Those who work most closely to information are the ones who best know why it is needed and how to manage it, so business units must be consulted in IG policy development. Business unit managers and analysts know their respective operations. Legal issues are the realm of in-house council and your legal team. The IT department understands its capabilities and technology plans and can best speak to those points. The records management department knows records. And cross-functional collaboration is needed for IG policies to hit the mark and be effective. The ultimate result will be not only more secure information but also better information to base decisions on and closer adherence to regulatory and legal demands.

2) Information policy development and communication. Clear policies must be established for the access and use of information, and those policies must be communicated regularly and crisply to employees. For instance, policies for the use of email, instant messaging, social media, cloud computing, mobile computing, and posting to blogs and internal sites must be developed in consultation with stakeholders and communicated clearly. This includes conveying clearly to employees what the consequences of violating IG policies are.

3) Information integrity. This area considers the consistency of methods used to create, retain, preserve, distribute, and track information. Adhering to good IG practices includes data governance techniques and technologies to ensure quality data. Information integrity means there is the assurance that information is accurate, correct, and authentic. IG efforts to improve data quality and information integrity include simply de-duplicating (removing redundant data) and maintaining only unique data to reduce risk, storage costs, and information technology (IT) labor costs while providing accurate, trusted information for decision makers. Supporting technologies must support enforcement of policies to meet legal standards of admissibility and preserve the integrity of information to guard against claims that it has been altered, tampered with, or deleted (called "**spoliation**"). Audit trails must be kept and monitored to ensure compliance with IG policies to assure information integrity.

4) Information organization and classification. This means standardizing formats, categorizing all information, and semantically linking it to related information. It also means creating a retention and disposition schedule that spells out how long the information (e.g. e-mail, e-documents, spreadsheets, reports) and records should be retained and how it is to be disposed of or archived. Information, and particularly documents, must be classified according to a global or corporate taxonomy that considers the business function and owner of the information, and also semantically linked to related information. Information must be standardized in form and format. Tools such as document labeling can assist in identifying and classifying e-documents. Metadata associated with documents and records must be standardized and kept up-to-date. Good IG means good metadata management and utilizing metadata standards that are appropriate to the organization.

5) Information security and privacy. This means securing information in its three states: at rest, in motion, and in use. It means implementing measures to protect information from damage, theft, or alteration by malicious outsiders and insiders as well as non-malicious (accidental) actions that may compromise information. For instance, an employee may lose a laptop with confidential information, but if proper IG policies are enforced using security-related information technologies, the information can be kept secure. This can be done by access control methods, data or document encryption, deploying information rights management software, using remote digital shredding capabilities, and implementing enhanced auditing procedures. Information privacy is another consideration closely related to information security and is critical when dealing with personally identifiable information (PII), protected health information (PHI), and other sensitive information.

6) Information accessibility. Accessibility is vital not only in the short term but also over time using long-term digital preservation (LTDP) techniques when appropriate (generally, if information is needed for over five years). Accessibility must be balanced with information security concerns. Information accessibility includes making the information as simple as possible to locate and access, which involves not only the user interface but also enterprise search principles, technologies, and tools. It also includes basic access controls, such as password management, identity and access management (IAM), and delivering information to a variety of hardware devices.

7) Information control. Document management, data management, and report management software must be deployed to control the access to, creation, updating, and printing of data, documents and reports. When information is declared a business record, it must be assigned to the proper retention and disposition schedule to be retained for as long as the records are needed to comply with legal retention periods and regulatory requirements. Also, non-record information must be classified and scheduled. And information that may be needed or requested in legal proceedings must be preserved and safeguarded through a legal hold process.

8) Information governance monitoring and auditing. To ensure that guidelines and policies are being followed and to measure employee compliance levels, information access and use must be monitored. To guard against claims of spoliation, the use of e-mail, social media, cloud computing, and report generation should be logged in real time and maintained as an audit record. Technology tools such as document analytics can track how many documents users access and print and how long they spend doing so.

9) Executive sponsorship. Once again, this is the most crucial factor in IG program success. No IG effort will survive and be successful if it does not have an accountable, responsible executive sponsor. The sponsor must drive the effort, clear obstacles for the IG team or steering committee, communicate the goals and business objectives that the IG program addresses, and keep upper management informed on progress particularly when accomplishing milestones.

10) Continuous improvement. IG programs are not one-time projects but rather ongoing programs that must be reviewed periodically and adjusted to account for gaps or shortcomings as well as changes in the business environment, technology usage, or business strategy.

If you are currently planning or implementing an IG program, these 10 principles are a good way to communicate with your stakeholders and IG steering committee what IG is, how it should be done, and how to fashion IG programs that succeed. You should continually reinforce the importance of these principles during the course of your IG program, and measure how well your organization is doing in these 10 critical areas.

CHAPTER SUMMARY: **KEY POINTS**

- **Cross-functional collaboration is needed for IG policies to hit the mark and be effective.**
- Lines of authority, accountability, & responsibility must be clear for the IG program to succeed.
- Adhering to good IG practices include data governance techniques and technologies to ensure quality data.
- Information form and formats should be standardized and classified according to a corporate taxonomy
- Sensitive information must be secure its three states: at rest, in motion, and in use.
- Privacy considerations should be injected into daily business processes.
- Information accessibility includes making it as simple as possible to locate and access info.
- Deploy software to control the access to, creation, updating, and printing of information.
- Information access and use must be monitored and audited.
- No IG effort will survive and be successful if it does not have an accountable, responsible executive sponsor.
- IG programs are not one-time projects but rather ongoing programs.

Chapter 9

Information Risk Planning & Management

Information risk planning involves identifying potential risks to information, weighing those risks, and creating strategic plans to mitigate the risks. Then your team develops those plans into specific policies, developing metrics to measure compliance levels, and identifying those who are accountable for executing the new risk mitigating processes. These processes must be audited and tested periodically not only to ensure compliance, but also to fine tune and provide feedback to improve the processes.

Depending on the jurisdiction, information is required to be retained by specific laws and regulations for specified periods, and to be produced in specified situations. To determine which laws and regulations apply to your organization's information, research into the legal and regulatory requirements for information in the jurisdictions in which you operate must be conducted.

Step 1: Survey and Determine Legal and Regulatory Applicability and Requirements

There are federal, provincial, state, and even municipal laws and regulations that may apply to the retention of information. Organizations operating in multiple jurisdictions must maintain compliance with laws and regulations that may cross national, state, or provincial boundaries. Legally required privacy requirements and retention periods must be researched for each jurisdiction (state, country) in which the business operates, so that it complies with all applicable laws.

Legal counsel and records managers (or your IG lead) must conduct their own legislative research to apprise themselves of mandatory information retention requirements, as well as privacy considerations and requirements, especially in regard to personally identifiable information (PII) and protected health information (PHI). This information must be analyzed and structured and then presented to legal staff for discussion. Then further legal and regulatory research must be conducted, and firm legal opinions must be rendered by your legal counsel regarding information retention, privacy and security requirements in accordance with laws and regulations. This is an absolute requirement. Your legal staff or outside legal counsel should provide input as to the legal hold process, provide opinions and interpretations of law that applies to your organization, and to provide input on the value of formal records, to arrive at a consensus on records that have legal value to the organization, and to construct an appropriate retention schedule.

Legal requirements trump all others. The retention period for a particular type of document or PII data or records series must meet minimum retention, privacy, and security requirements as mandated by law. Business needs and other considerations are secondary. So, legal research is required before determining and implementing retention periods, privacy policies, and security measures." In identifying information requirements and risks, legal requirements trump all others.

In order to locate the regulations and citations relating to retention of records, there are two basic approaches. The first approach is to use a Records Retention Citation Service, which publishes in electronic form all of the retention-related citations. These services are usually purchased on a subscription basis, as the citations are updated on an annual or more frequent basis as legislation and regulations change.

94

Another approach is to search the laws and regulations directly using online or print resources. Records retention requirements for corporations operating in the United States may be found in the **Code of Federal Regulations (CFR).** "The Code of Federal Regulations (CFR) annual edition is the codification of the general and permanent rules published in the Federal Register by the departments and agencies of the federal government. It is divided into 50 titles that represent broad areas subject to federal regulation."[26]

For governmental agencies, a key consideration is complying with requests for information as a result of the U.S. Freedom of Information Act (FOIA), Freedom of Information Act 2000 (in the U.K.), and similar legislation in other countries. So the process of governing information is critical to meeting these requests by the public for governmental records.

Step 2: Specify IG Requirements to Achieve Compliance

Once the legal research has been conducted, and a process for keeping updated on laws and regulations has been established, specific external compliance requirements can be listed and those data, document, and record sets that apply to those external compliance requirements can be mapped back to applicable data sets, document collections, and records series. The crucial task is keeping apprised of changes and updating the policies and processes appropriately.

Internal IG policies may be different that than the legally-mandated minimums. For instance, an organization that is not operating in a highly regulated industry has more flexibility. They may want to balance defensible deletion with a need to grow corporate memory and develop "knowledge bases." They would have the option to dispose of email that is not cited for legal hold after 90 days, but may choose, based on corporate culture and other business factors, to retain email messages for six months, or a year. Similarly, the organization may make legally defensible

95

deletion decisions that reduce the total amount of information it must manage by using a "last accessed" rationale, whereby information that has not been accessed for over one year (or whatever the specified period is) may be destroyed and discarded, as a matter of policy.

Step 3: Create a Risk Profile

Creating a **risk profile** is a basic building block in **enterprise risk management** (yet *another* "ERM"), which assists executives in understanding the risks associated with stated business objectives, and allocating resources, within a structured evaluation approach or framework. There are multiple ways to create a risk profile, and how often it is done, the external sources consulted and stakeholders who have input will vary from organization to organization.[27] A key tenet to bear in mind is that *simpler is better*, and that sophisticated tools and techniques should not make the process overly complex. According to ISO, risk is defined as "the effect of uncertainty on objectives" and **a risk profile is "a description of a set of risks."**[28] Creating a risk profile involves identifying, documenting, assessing, and prioritizing risks that an organization may face in pursuing its business objectives. Those associated risks can be evaluated and delineated within a risk or IG framework.

The corporate risk profile should be an informative tool for executive management, the CEO, and the board of directors, so it should reflect that tone. In other words, it should be clear, succinct, and simplified. A risk profile may also serve to inform the head of a division or subsidiary, in which case it may contain more detail. The process is applicable and can also be applied to public and nonprofit entities.

The time horizon for a risk profile varies, but looking out three to five years is a good rule of thumb.[29] The risk profile typically will be created annually, although semi-annually would serve the organization better and account for changes in the business and legal environment. But if an organization is competing in a market sector with rapid business cycles or volatility, the risk profile should be generated more frequently, perhaps quarterly.

There are different types of risk profile methodologies, with a "**Top Ten**" list, **risk map**, and **heat map**, being commonly used. The first is a simple identification and ranking of the ten greatest risks in relation to business objectives. The risk map is a visual tool that is easy to grasp, with a grid depicting a likelihood axis and an impact axis, usually rated on a scale of 1-5. In a risk assessment meeting, stakeholders can weigh in on risks using voting technology to generate a consensus. A heat map is a color-coded matrix generated by stakeholders voting on risk level by color (e.g. red being highest).

Information gathering is a fundamental activity in building the risk profile. Surveys are good for gathering basic information, but for more detail, a good method to employ is direct, person-to-person interviews, beginning with executives and risk professionals.[30] Select a representative cross section of functional groups to gain a broad view. Depending on the size of the organization, you may need to conduct 20-40 interviews, with one person asking the questions and probing, while another team member takes notes and asks occasionally for clarification or elaboration. Conduct the interviews in a compressed timeframe—knock them out within one to three weeks and do not drag the process out, as business conditions and personnel can change over the course of months.

There are a number of helpful considerations to conducting successful interviews. First, prepare some questions for the interviewee in advance, so they may prepare and do some of their own research. Secondly, schedule the interview close to their office, and at their convenience. Thirdly, keep the time as short as possible, but long enough to get the answers you will need; approximately 20-45 minutes. Be sure to leave some open time between interviews to collect your thoughts and prepare for the next one. And follow up with interviewees after analyzing and distilling the notes to confirm you have gained the correct insights.

The information you will be harvesting will vary depending on the interviewee's level and function. You will need to look for any hard data or reports that show performance and trends related to information risk. There may be benchmarking data available as well. Delve into information access and security policies, policy development, policy adherence, and the like. Ask questions about retention of email and legal hold processes. Ask about records retention and disposition policies. Ask about long term preservation of digital records. Ask about their data deletion policies. Ask for documentation regarding IG-related training and communications. Dig into policies for access to confidential data and vital records. Try to get a real sense of the way things are run, what is standard operating procedure, and also how workers might get around overly restrictive policies, or operate without clear policies. Learn enough so that you can grasp the management style and corporate culture, and then distill that information into your findings.

Key events and developments must also be included in the risk profile. For instance, a major data breach, the loss or potential loss of a major lawsuit, pending regulatory changes that could impact your IG policies, or a change in business ownership or structure must all be accounted for and factored into the information risk profile. Even changes in governmental leadership should be considered, if they might impact IG policies. These types of developments should be tracked on a regular basis, and should continue to feed into the risk equation.[31] You must observe and incorporate an analysis of key events in developing and updating the risk profile.

At this point, it should be possible to generate a list of specific potential risks. It may be useful to group or categorize the potential risks into clusters such as natural disaster, regulatory, safety, competitive, and so forth. Armed with this list of risks, you should solicit input from stakeholders as to likelihood and timing of the threats or risks. As the organization matures in its risk identification and handling capabilities, a good practice is to look at the risks and their ratings from the previous years to attempt to gain insights into change and trends—both external and internal—that affected the risks.

Step 4: Perform Risk Analysis and Assessment

Once you have created a risk profile and identified key risks, an assessment of the likelihood that these risks hold and their resultant impact must be done.

There are five basic steps in conducting a risk assessment:[32]

1) **Identify the risks** – this should be an output of creating a risk profile, but if conducting a risk assessment, first identify the major information-related risks.

2) **Determine potential impact** – if a calculation of a range of economic impact is possible (e.g. lose $5M-$10M in legal damages), then include it. If not, be as specific as possible as to how a negative event related to an identified risk can impact business objectives.

3) **Evaluate risk levels and probabilities and recommend action** – this may be in the form of recommending new procedures or processes, new investments in information technology, or other actions to mitigate identified risks.

4) **Create a report with recommendations and implement** - you may want to include a risk assessment table as well as written recommendations, then implement.

5) **Review periodically** – annually or semi-annually, as appropriate for your organization.

A helpful exercise and visual tool is to draw up a table of top risks, their potential impact, and actions that have been taken to mitigate the risk.

Step 5: Develop an Information Risk Mitigation Plan

After setting out the risks, their potential impact, and suggested countermeasures for mitigation, you must create the **information risk mitigation plan**, which means developing risk mitigation options and tasks to reduce the specified risks and improve the odds of achieving business objectives.[33]You assemble the documentation you have collected and analyzed in creating the risk profile and risk assessment, and assign specifics. The information risk mitigation plan should include a timetable and milestones for implementation of the recommended risk mitigation measures, including IT acquisition and implementation, and assigning roles and responsibilities, such as executive sponsor, project manager (PM), and project team.

Step 6: Develop Metrics and Measure Results

To measure conformance and performance of your IG program, you must have an objective way to measure how you are doing, which means numbers, metrics. Assigning some quantitative measures that are meaningful and do, in fact, measure progress may take some serious effort and consultation with stakeholders. Determining relevant ways of measuring progress will allow executives to see progress, as, realistically, *reducing risk is not something anyone can see or feel*—it is only in the failure to do so, when the risk comes home to roost, when the painful realizations are made. Also, valid metrics help to justify investment in the IG program.

The proper metrics will vary from organization to organization. Below are some examples of specific metrics:

- Reduce the data lost on stolen or misplaced laptops by 50% over the previous fiscal year

100

- Reduce the number of hacker intrusion events by 75% over the previous fiscal year

- Reduce e-discovery costs by 25% over the previous fiscal year

- Reduce the number of adverse findings in the risk and compliance audit by 50% over the previous fiscal year

- Roll out the implementation of encryption software to protect sensitive information to 50 users this fiscal year

- Provide confidential messaging services for the organization's 20 top executives this fiscal year

Your organization's IG Program metrics should be tailored and should tie directly to stated business objectives.

Step 7: Execute Your Risk Mitigation Plan

Now you have the risk mitigation plan, it must be executed. This means that you must set up regular project team meetings, develop key reports on your information risk mitigation metrics, and manage the process. This is done using proven project and program management tools and techniques, which you may want to supplement with collaboration software tools, knowledge management software, or even social media.

However, most importantly it involves communicating clearly and regularly with the IG team on the progress and status of the IG effort to reduce information risk.

Step 8: Audit the Information Risk Mitigation Program

Using the metrics you have developed, put a process in place to independently audit compliance with risk mitigation measures, to see that they are being implemented. The result of the audit should be a useful input in improving and fine-tuning the program. It should not be viewed so much as an opportunity to cite shortfalls and implement punitive actions. It should be a periodic and regular feedback loop into the IG program.

CHAPTER SUMMARY: **KEY POINTS**

- **In identifying information requirements and risks, legal requirements trump all others.**
- The risk profile is a high-level, executive decision input tool which helps to gauge risks.
- A common risk profile method is to create a prioritized or ranked "Top Ten" list of greatest risks to information.
- Once a list of risks is developed, grouping them into basic categories helps stakeholders.
- The risk mitigation plan develops risk reduction options and tasks to reduce specified risks.
- Metrics are required to measure progress in the risk mitigation plan.

Chapter 10

Strategic Planning and Best Practices for IG

Align Your IG Plan with Strategic Plans

The IG plan must support the achievement of the organization's business objectives, and therefore must be melded into the overall strategic plan for the organization. Integration with the strategic plan means that pursuing the business objectives in the IG plan are consistent with, and in support of, the enterprise strategic plan.

So, for example, if the corporate strategy includes plans for acquiring smaller competitors and folding them into the organization's structure as operating divisions, then the IG plan must assist and contribute to this effort. Plans for standardizing operating policies and procedures amongst the new acquisitions must include a consistent, systematized approach to key principles of IG, including stakeholder consultation, user training and communications, and compliance audits. The IG plan should bring a standard approach across the spectrum of information use and management within the organization and must be forged to accommodate the new acquisitions. This means that email policies, e-discovery policies, mobile device policies, social media policies, cloud collaboration and storage use, and even nitty gritty details like report formats, data structures, document taxonomies and metadata, must be consistent and aligned with the overall strategic plan. In other words, the goal is to get all employees on the "same page" and working to support the business objectives of the strategic plan in everyday small steps within the IG plan.

The organization will also have an IT plan, which must be aligned with the strategic plan to support overall business objectives. The IT strategy may be to convert new acquisitions to the internal financial and accounting systems of the organization, and to train newly-acquired employees to use the existing software applications under the umbrella of the IG plan. Or the IT plan may be to move to cloud computing. Again, the IG plan needs to be integrated with the IT strategy and must consider the organization's approach to IT.

The result of the process of aligning the IG effort with the IT strategy and the organization's overall strategic plan will mean, ideally, that employee efforts are more efficient and productive since they are consistently moving toward the achievement of the organization's overall strategic goals. The organization will be healthier, and will have less dissent and confusion, with clear IG policies that leverage the IT strategy and help pursue overall business objectives.

There are further considerations that must be folded into the IG plan. As every corporate culture is different, and has a real impact on decision-making and operational approaches, it must be considered. Corporate culture includes the organization's appetite for risk, its use of IT (e.g. forward thinking "first adopter"), its capital investment strategies, and other management actions.

So, if the organization is conservative and risk averse, it may want to hold off on implementing some emerging e-discovery technologies than can cut costs but also induce greater risk. Or, if it is an aggressive, progressive, risk-taking organization, it may opt to test and adopt newer e-discovery technologies, under the

IT strategy, and umbrella of IG policies. An example may be the use of predictive coding technology in early case assessment (ECA). Predictive coding uses text auto-classification technology and neural technology with the assistance of human input to "learn" which e-documents might be responsive in a particular legal matter, and which may not be. Through a series of steps of testing and checking subsets of the documents, human experts provide input to improve the sorting and selection process. The software uses machine learning (artificial intelligence whereby the software can change and improve on a particular task, as its decision engine is shaped and "trained" by input) to improve its ability to cull through and sort documents.

Predictive coding can reduce e-discovery costs, yet there are risks that the approach can be challenged in court and could, in fact, affect the case adversely. So it is clear to see how a decision on a technology like predictive coding can involve and include elements of the IG plan, IT strategy, and overall organizational strategic plan.

And there are resource issues to consider: how much management time or "bandwidth" is available to pursue the IG plan development and execution? Is there a budget item to allow for software acquisitions and training and communications to support the execution of the IG plan? Obviously, without the allocated management time, and budget money, the IG plan cannot be executed.

Survey and Evaluate External Factors

The IG plan is now harmonized and aligned with your organization's strategic plan and IT strategy, but you are not finished yet, because it cannot survive in a vacuum: organizations

Analyze Information Technology Trends

IG requires IT to support and monitor implementation of polices, so it matters what is developing and trending in the information technology space. What new technologies are coming online? Why are they being developed and becoming popular? How do these changes in the business environment that created opportunities for new technologies to be developed affect your organization and its ability execute its IG plan? How can new technologies assist? Which ones are immature and too risky? These are some of the questions that must be addressed in regard to the changing information technology landscape.

Some changes in information and communications technology (ICT) are rather obvious, such as the trends toward mobile computing, tablet and smartphone devices, cloud storage, and social media use. Each one of these major trends that may affect or assist in implementing IG needs to be considered, and again, this must be done within the framework of the organization's strategic plan and IT strategy. If the corporate culture is progressive and supportive of remote work and telecommuting, and the organizational strategy aims to lower fixed costs by reducing the amount of fixed office space for employees and moving to a more mobile workforce, then trends in tablet and smartphone computing that are relevant to your organization must be analyzed and considered. Is the organization going to provide mobile devices, or support a bring-your-own-device (BYOD) environment? Which equipment will you support? Will you support iOS, Android, or both? What is your policy going to be on phone jacking/modification? What is the IG policy regarding confidential documents on mobile devices? Will you use encryption? If so, which software? Is your enterprise moving to the cloud computing model? Utilizing social media? What about Big Data? Are you going to consider deploying auto-

must analyze and consider the external business, legal, and technological environment and fold their analysis into their plans.

classification and predictive coding technologies? What are the trends that might affect your organization?

There are many, many questions that must be addressed, but the evaluation must be narrowed down to those technology trends that specifically might impact the execution of your IG plan, and rollout of new technology.

On a more granular level, you must evaluate even supported file and document formats. It gets that detailed, when you are crafting IG policy. For instance, PDF/A is the standard format for archiving electronic documents. So your plans must include long term digital preservation (LTDP) standards and best practices.

Survey Business Conditions and Economic Environment

If the economy is on a down cycle, and particularly if your business sector has been negatively affected, resources may be scarcer than in better times, and hence, it may be more difficult to get budget approval for necessary program expenses, such as new technologies, staff, contractors, training materials, and so forth. This means your IG plan may need to be scaled back, or its scope reduced. Implementing the plan in a key division rather than attempting an enterprise rollout is the best tact in tough economic times, and at all times, really. Start small.

But if things are booming, and the business is growing fast, then budget money for investments in the IG program may be easier to secure, and the goals may be expanded.

IG should be an ongoing program, but it takes time to implement, and it takes resources to execute, audit and continue to refine. So an executive looking for a quick and calculable payback on the investment may want to focus on narrower areas. For instance, the focus may be entirely on the legal hold and e-discovery process initially, with business objectives that include reducing pre-trial costs and attorney fees by a certain percentage or amount. It is much easier to see concrete results when focusing on e-discovery, since legal costs are real, and will always be there. However, if the IG effort is broader and improves the ability to organize and search for information faster, and to execute more complete searches to improve the basis for management decision-making, the business case may be more difficult to make. Improved management decision-making will improve the organization's competitiveness long-term, but it may be difficult to cite specific examples where costs were saved or revenues were increased as a result of the "better decisions" that should come about through better information governance.

Analyze relevant legal, regulatory, and political factors

In consultation with your legal team or lead, the laws and regulations that affect your industry should be identified. Narrowing the scope of your analysis, those that specifically could impact your governance of information should be considered and analyzed. What absolute requirements do they impose? Where there is room for interpretation, where, legally, does your organization want to position itself? How much legal risk is acceptable? These are the types of questions you will have to look to your legal and risk management professionals to make. Again, legal requirements trump all others.

Your decision process must include considerations for the future, and anticipated future changes. Changes in the legal and regulatory environment happen based on the political leaders who are in place, and any pending legislation. Therefore, you must go further and analyze the current political environment, and make some judgments based on the best information you can gather, the organization's culture and appetite for risk, management style, available resources, and other factors. Generally, a more conservative environment means less regulation, and this analysis must also be folded into your IG strategic plan.

Survey and Determine Industry Best Practices

Information governance is a developing hybrid "super discipline" that is a superset of infosec and records management and e-discovery and data governance that emerged to help manage the explosion in the amount of information that must be managed in today's increasingly regulated and litigious business environment. As such, Best Practices are still being formed and expanded. This process of testing, proving, and sharing best practices will continue for the next decade as Best Practices are expanded, revised, and refined.

The most relevant study of IG Best Practices is one that is conducted for your organization which surveys your industry and even what some of your more progressive competitors are doing in regard to IG. Often, engaging a third party consultant is the best way to get this accomplished, since they can more easily contact, study and interview your competitors' practices. But also, there are business peer groups and trade associations which can provide some consensus as to emerging best practices.

Below is a sampling of IG Best Practices that cover a number of areas where IG has an impact or should be a major consideration. These are a starting point; you must search for Best Practices within your own industry and within your organization to customize them and make them meaningful guidelines to drive your IG effort:

1. **IG is a key underpinning for a successful E-records Management program**—Practicing good IG is the essential foundation for building a legally defensible records management program; it provides the basis for consistent, reliable methods for managing documents and records. Having trusted and reliable records, reports and databases allow managers to make key decisions with confidence.[34]And accessing that information and business intelligence in a timely fashion can yield a long-term sustainable competitive advantage, creating more agile enterprises.

109

To do this, enterprises must standardize and systematize their handling of information, and most especially their formal business records. They must analyze and optimize how information is accessed, controlled, managed, shared, stored, preserved, and audited. They must have complete, current, and relevant policies, processes, and technologies to manage and control information, including who is able to access what information, and when, to meet external legal and regulatory demands and internal governance requirements. This, in short, is IG.

2. **IG is not a project but rather an ongoing program** that provides an umbrella of rules and policies, monitored and enforced with the support of information technologies to manage and control information output and communications. Since technologies change so quickly, it is necessary to have overarching "technology agnostic" policies to manage the various IT platforms that an organization may use.

   Compare it to a workplace safety program; every time a new location, team member, piece of equipment, or toxic substance is acquired by the organization, the workplace safety program should dictate how that is handled and, if it doesn't, workplace safety policies/procedures/training need to be updated. And you monitor and audit and conduct regular reviews to ensure the program is followed and make adjustments based on your findings. The effort never ends.[35]

3. **Using an IG framework or maturity model is helpful in assessing and guiding IG programs**—various models are offered, such as the Generally Accepted Recordkeeping Principles®("The Principles") from ARMA International; the Information Governance Reference Model (IGRM) which grew out of the Electronic Discovery Reference Model (found at EDRM.net)[36] or MIKE2.0, which was developed by Bearing Point and released to the public domain.

4. **An enterprise-wide retention schedule is preferable**

because it eliminates the possibility that different business units will be following conflicting records retention periods. For example, if one business unit is discarding a group of records after five years, it would not make sense for another business unit to keep the same records for 10 years. Where enterprise-wide retention schedules are not possible, then smaller business units, such as divisions or regions, should operate under a consistent retention schedule.

5. **Senior management must set the tone** and lead sponsorship for vital records program governance and compliance**.** Although e-records are easier to protect and backup, and most vital records today are e-records, without vital records, an organization cannot continue operations.

6. **Business processes must be redesigned to improve the management of electronic records** or implement an electronic records management (ERM) system. Using ERM fundamentally changes the way people work, and greater efficiencies can be gained with business process redesign (versus simply using ERM systems as an electronic filing cabinet).

7. **E-mail messages, both inbound and outbound, should be archived automatically and (preferably) in real-time.** This ensures that spoliation does not occur, that is, the loss of proven authenticity of an e-mail. This preserves legal validity and forensic compliance. Additionally, e-mail should be indexed to facilitate the searching process, and all messages should be secured in a single location. With these measures, e-mail records can be assured to be authentic and reliable.

8. **Personal archiving of e-mail messages should be disallowed.** Although users will want to save certain e-mail messages for their own reasons, control and management of e-mail archiving must be at the organization level, or as high of a level as is practical, such as division or region.

9. **Destructive retention of e-mail helps to reduce storage**

costs and legal risk, while improving "findability" of critical
records. It makes good business sense to have a policy to,
say, destroy all e-mail messages after 90 or 120 days that are
not flagged as potential records or those that have a legal
hold.

10. Take a practical approach and limit cloud use to documents
that do not have long retention periods and carry a low
litigation risk—this will reduce the risk of compromising or
losing critical documents and e-records. Some duplicate
copies of vital records may be stored securely in the cloud to
help the organization recover in the event of a disaster.

11. Social media content must be managed by IG policies and
monitored with controls that ensure protection of critical
information assets, and preservation of business records.
Your organization must state clearly what content and tone
is acceptable in social media use, and it must retain records
of that use, which should be captured in real-time.

12. International and national standards provide effective
guidance for implementing IG. Although there are no
absolutes, researching and referencing ISO and other
standards must be a part of any IG effort.

13. Creating standardized metadata terms should be part of an
IG effort that enables faster, more complete, and more
accurate searches and retrieval of records. This is important
not only in everyday business operations, but also when
delving through potentially millions of records during the
discovery phase of litigation. Good metadata management
also assists in the maintenance of corporate memory, and
improving accountability in business operations.[37]Using a
standardized format and controlled vocabulary provides a
"precise and comprehensible description of content,
location, and value."[38] Using a controlled vocabulary means
your organization has standardized a set of terms used for
metadata elements describing records. This "ensures
consistency across a collection" and helps with optimizing
search and retrieval functions and records research, as well

as meeting e-discovery requests, compliance demands, and other legal and regulatory requirements.

14. **Some digital information assets must be preserved permanently as part of an organization's documentary heritage.**[39]Long-term digital preservation (LTDP) applies to content that is born digital as well as content that is converted to digital form. Digital preservation is defined as: long-term, error-free storage of digital information, with means for retrieval and interpretation, for the entire time span that the information is required to be retained. Dedicated repositories for historical and cultural memory such as libraries, archives, and museums, need to move forward to put in place trustworthy digital repositories that can match the security, environmental controls, and wealth of descriptive metadata that these institutions have created for analog assets (such as books and paper records). Digital challenges associated with records management affect all sectors of society—academic, government, private, and not-for-profit enterprises—and ultimately all citizens of all developed nations.

15. **Executive sponsorship is crucial.** Securing an executive sponsor at the senior management level is key to successful IG projects and programs. It is not possible to require managers to take time out of their other duties to participate in a project if there is no executive edict. It is a best practice and supports the Generally Accepted Recordkeeping Principles® Accountability principle.[40]

Formulating the IG Strategic Plan

Now comes the time to make sense of all the data and input your IG team has gathered and hammer it into a workable IG strategic plan. This will involve some give-and-take amongst IG team members, each having their own perspective and priorities. Everyone will be lobbying for their functional groups view, but it is the job of the executive sponsor to set the tone. They must emphasize organizational business objectives so that the effort does not drag out or turn into a competition, but rather, a well-informed consensus development process that results in a clear, workable IG strategic plan.

Synthesize Gathered Information and Fuse Into IG Strategy

At this point your IG team will have gathered a great deal of information that needs to be analyzed and distilled into actionable strategies. This process will depend on the expertise and input of the specialized knowledge your team brings to the table within the construct of your organizational culture. They must be able to make decisions and establish priorities that bear in mind organizational business objectives and consider a number of influencing factors.

Do not prolong the strategy development process; the longer it becomes, the more key factors influencing it can change.

You want to develop a strategic plan that is durable enough to withstand changes in technology, legislation, and other key influencing factors, but it should be relevant to that snapshot of information that was collected early on. When all the parts and pieces start changing, and require reconsideration, it does not serve the organization well.

Develop IG strategies for each of the critical areas, including the legal hold process, e-discovery action plans, email policy, mobile computing policy, IT acquisition strategy, confidential document handling, vital records and disaster planning, social media policy, and other areas that are important to your organization. Do this first without regard to the prioritization of these areas to maintain focus.

Then you must go through the hard process of prioritizing your strategies, and aligning them to your organizational goal and objectives. This may not be difficult in the beginning. For instance, your IG strategies for legal holds and e-discovery readiness are likely going to take higher priority than your social media policy, and protecting vital records is paramount to any organization, but as the process progresses it will become more challenging to make tradeoffs and establish priorities. Then you must tie these strategies to overall organizational goals and business objectives.

A good technique to keep goals and objectives in mind may be to post them prominently in the meeting room where these strategy sessions take place. This will help to keep the IG team focused.

Develop Actionable Plans to Support Organizational Goals and Objectives

Plans and policies to support your IG efforts must be developed that identify specific tasks and steps, and define roles and responsibilities for those who will be held accountable for their implementation. This is where the rubber meets the road. But you cannot simply create the plan and marching orders: you must build in periodic checks and audits to test that new IG policies are being followed, and that they have hit their mark. Invariably, there will be adjustments, and the adjustments must be continually made to craft the policies for maximum effectiveness, and continued relevance in the face of changes in external factors such as legislation and business competition, and internal changes in management style and structure.

Create New IG Driving Programs to Support Business Goals and Objectives

You've got to get things moving, get employees motivated, and launching new sub-programs within the overall IG program is a good way to start. For instance, a new "E-discovery readiness" initiative can show almost immediate results if implemented properly, with the support of key legal and records management team members, driven by the executive sponsor. You may want to revamp the **legal hold notification** (LHN) process to make it more complete and verifiable, assigning specific employees specific tasks to be accountable for. Part of that effort may be evaluating and implementing new technology assisted review (TAR) processes and predictive coding technology. So you will need to bring in the IG team members responsible for IT, and perhaps business analysis. Working cooperatively on smaller parts of the overall IG program is a way to show real results within defined timeframes. Piecing together a series of program components is the best way to get started and it breaks the overall IG program down into digestible, doable chunks. A small win early on is crucial to maintain momentum and executive sponsorship. And e-discovery has real costs, so progress can be measured objectively in terms of reducing the cost of activities such as early case assessment (ECA). Benefits can be measured in terms of reduced attorney review hours, reduced costs, and reduced time to accomplish pre-trial tasks.

To be clear you will need to negotiate and agree on the success metrics the program will be measured on in advance.

There are other examples of supporting IG sub-programs, such as email management and archiving, where storage costs, search times, and information breaches can be measured in objective terms. Or you may choose to roll out new policies for the use of mobile devices within your organization, where adherence to policy can be measure by scanning mobile devices and monitoring their use.

Draft the IG Strategic Plan and Gain Input from a Broader Group of Stakeholders

Once you have the pieces of the plan drafted, and the IG team is in agreement that it has been harmonized and aligned with overall organizational goals and objectives, you must test the waters to see if you have hit the mark. So it is a good practice to expose a broader group of stakeholders to the plan to gain their input. Perhaps your IG team has become myopic, or has passed over some points that are important to the broader stakeholder audience. So solicit and discuss their input, and to the degree that there is a consensus, refine the IG strategic plan one last time before finalizing it. But remember, it is a living document, a work-in-progress, which will require revisiting and updating to assure it is in step with changing external and internal factors. Periodic auditing and review of the plan will reveal areas that need to be adjusted and revised to keep the plan relevant and effective.

Get Buy In and Sign Off and Execute the Plan

Take the finalized plan to executive management, preferably including the CEO, and present the plan and its intended benefits to them. Field their questions and address any concerns to gain their buy in, and the appropriate signatures. You may have to make some minor adjustments if there are significant objections, but, if you have executed the stakeholder consultation process properly, you show be very close to the mark. Then begin the process of implementing your IG strategic plan including regular status meetings and updates, steady communication and reassurance of your executive sponsor, and planned audits of activities.

CHAPTER SUMMARY: **KEY POINTS**

- Engaged and invested executive sponsors are necessary for IG program success. It is not possible to require managers to take time out of their other duties otherwise.

- The executive sponsor must be: (a) directly tied to the success of the program, (b) fully engaged and aware in the program, and (c) actively eliminating barriers and resolving issues.

- The role of the executive sponsor evolves over the life of the IG program.

- While the executive sponsor role is high level, the project manager's role and tasks are more detailed and day-to-day management.

- **The information risk mitigation plan develops risk reduction options and tasks to reduce specified risks and improve the odds for achieving business objectives.**

- The IG strategic plan must be aligned and synchronized with the organization's overall strategic plans, goals and business objectives.

- The IG strategic plan must be informed with an assessment of relevant technology trends.

- Include trends and conditions in the internal and external business environment.

- Laws and regulations relevant to your organization's management and distribution of information in all jurisdictions must be considered and included in the IG strategic plan.

- Legal requirements trump all others.
- Include a best practices review in your IG strategic plan. The most relevant best practices in IG are those in your industry proven by peers and competitors.
- Fuse the findings of all your analysis of external and internal factors into your IG strategic plan. Develop strategies and then prioritize them.
- Create supporting sub-programs to jump start your IG program effort. Smaller programs should be able to measure real results based upon metrics that are agreed upon in advance.
- Make sure to get executive sign off on your IG strategic plan before moving to execute it.

Robert Smallwood

Chapter 11

Information Governance Policy Development

To develop information governance (IG) policy, you must inform and frame the policy with internal and external frameworks, models, best practices and standards—those that apply to your organization and the scope of its planned IG program. In this section, we will first present and discuss key IG frameworks and models, and then move on to identify key standards for consideration.

A Brief Review of Generally Accepted Recordkeeping Principles®

In 2009, ARMA International published a set of eight Generally Accepted Recordkeeping Principles® known as "The Principles,"[41] (or sometimes "GAR Principles"). These principles and associated metrics provide an information governance (IG) framework that can support continuous improvement.

To review, the eight Generally Accepted Recordkeeping Principles are:

1. Accountability
2. Transparency
3. Integrity
4. Protection
5. Compliance

6. Availability

7. Retention

8. Disposition[42]

The Principles establish benchmarks for how organizations of all types and sizes can build and sustain compliant, legally defensible **records management** (RM) programs. Using the Maturity Model organizations can assess where they are in terms of IG, identify gaps, and take steps to improve across the eight areas The Principles cover.

The IG Reference Model (IGRM)

In late 2012, with the support and collaboration of ARMA International and CGOC (Compliance, Governance and Oversight Council), the Electronic Discovery Reference Model (EDRM) Project released version 3.0 of its Information Governance Reference Model (IGRM), which added **information privacy and security** "as primary functions and stakeholders in the effective governance of information." The model is depicted on the opposite page:

Information Governance Reference Model (IGRM)

Linking duty + value to information asset = efficient, effective management

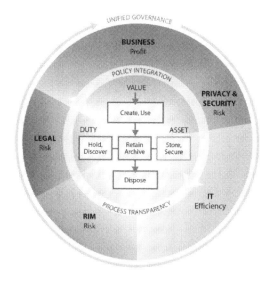

Duty: Legal obligation for specific information

Value: Utility or business purpose of specific information

Asset: Specific container of information

Source: EDRM.net.[43]

The IGRM is aimed at fostering IG adoption by facilitating communication and collaboration between disparate (but overlapping) IG stakeholder functions, including IT, legal, records management, risk management, and business unit stakeholders.[44] It also aims to provide a "common, practical framework" for IG that will foster adoption of IG in the face of new Big Data challenges and increased legal and regulatory demands. It is a clear snapshot of where IG touches and shows critical interrelationships and unified governance.[45] It can help organizations forge policy in an orchestrated way, and to embed critical elements of IG policy across functional groups. Ultimately, implementation of IG helps organizations leverage information value, reduce risk, and address legal demands.

Interpreting the IGRM Diagram[46]

The Outer Ring

Starting from the outside of the diagram, successful information management is about conceiving a complex set of interoperable processes, and implementing the procedures and structural elements to put them into practice. It requires:

- An understanding of the business imperatives of the enterprise,

- Knowledge of the appropriate tools and infrastructure for managing information, and

- Sensitivity to the legal and regulatory obligations with which the enterprise must comply.

For any piece of information one hopes to manage, the primary stakeholder is the business user of that information [italics added]. We use the term "business" broadly; the same ideas apply to end users of information in organizations whose ultimate goal might not be to generate a profit.

Once the business value is established, one must also understand the legal duty attached to a piece of information. The term "legal" should also be read broadly to refer to a wide range of legal and regulatory constraints and obligations, from e-discovery and government regulation, to contractual obligations such as payment card industry requirements.

Finally, IT organizations must manage the information accordingly, ensuring privacy and security as well as appropriate retention as dictated by both business and legal or regulatory requirements.

The business user is the primary stakeholder of managed information.

The Center

In the center of the diagram is a workflow, or lifecycle diagram. We include this component in the diagram to illustrate the fact that information management is important at all stages of the information lifecycle – from its creation through its ultimate disposition. This part of the diagram, once further developed, along with other secondary level diagrams, will outline concrete, actionable steps that organizations can take in implementing information management programs.

Even the most primitive business creates information in the course of daily operations, and IT departments spring up to manage the logistics – indeed, one of the biggest challenges in modern organizations is trying to stop individuals from excess storing and securing of information. Legal stakeholders can usually mandate the preservation of what is most critical, though often at great cost. However, it takes the coordinated effort of all three groups to defensibly dispose of a piece of information that has outlived its usefulness, and retain what IS useful in a way that enables accessibility and usability for the business user.

How the IGRM Complements the Generally Accepted Recordkeeping Principles®[47]

The IGRM supports ARMA International's "The Principles" by identifying the cross-functional groups of key information governance stakeholders and by depicting their intersecting objectives for the organization. This illustration of the relationship between duty, value and the information asset demonstrates cooperation among stakeholder groups to achieve the desired level of maturity of effective information governance.

Effective IG requires a continuous and comprehensive focus. The IGRM will be used by proactive organizations as an introspective lens to facilitate visualization and discussion about how best to apply the GAR Principles. The IGRM puts into sharp focus the GAR Principles and provides essential context for the Maturity Model.

Best Practices Considerations

IG best practices should also be considered in policy formulation. Best practices in IG are evolving and expanding, and those that apply to organizational scenarios may vary. So a best practices review should be conducted, customized for each particular organization.

In the previous chapter we provided a list of IG best practices, with some detail. It should be emphasized that these are only a partial list in the maturing IG world, and that these best practices are fairly generic and widely-applicable. You will need to customize them for your organization. A more extensive list may be found in *Information Governance: Concepts, Strategies, and Best Practices* (Wiley, 2014) by Robert Smallwood. But you and your team will need to craft your own set of best practices by selecting those you feel apply to your organization, and from peer interviews and research. A consulting firm may have benchmarking data and can assist in developing best practices for your organization. These best practices will help guide your IG program efforts.

Key Standards Relevant to IG Efforts

Below we introduce and discuss some established standards that should be researched and considered as a foundation for developing IG policy.

Risk Management

ISO 31000:2009 is a broad, industry-agnostic (not specific to vertical markets) risk management standard. It states "principles and generic guidelines" of risk management that can be applied to not only IG but also to a wide range of organizational activities and processes throughout the life of an organization.[48]

Information Security

ISO/IEC 27001:2005 is an Information Security Management System standard that provides guidance in the development of security controls to safeguard information assets.[49]

ISO/IEC 27002: 2005—"Information Technology—Security Techniques—Code of Practice for Information Security[50]establishes guidelines and general principles for initiating, implementing, maintaining, and improving information security management in an organization.

Records and E-records Management

ISO 15489–1:2001 is the international standard for records management (RM). It identifies the elements of RM and provides a framework and high-level overview of RM core principles.

ISO 30300 series: In November 2011, ISO issued new standards for Electronic Records Management, the first two in the ISO 30300 series, which are based on a *managerial* point of view and targeted at a management-level audience, rather than for records managers or technical staff:

- **ISO 30300:2011.** "Information and Documentation—Management Systems for Records—Fundamentals and Vocabulary"

- **ISO 30301:2011.** "Information and Documentation—Management Systems for Records—Requirements"

The ISO 30300 series is a systematic approach to the creation and management of records that is "aligned with organizational objectives and strategies.[51]

IT Security and Governance

ISO/IEC 38500:2008 is an international standard that provides high level principles and guidance for senior executives and directors, and those advising them, for the effective and efficient use of IT.[52] It "applies to the governance of management processes" which are performed at the IT service level but the guidance assists executives in monitoring IT and ethically discharging their duties with respect to legal and regulatory compliance of IT activities.[53]

Business Continuity Management (BCM)

ISO 22301:2012, "Societal Security – Business Continuity Management Systems – Requirements" spells out the requirements for creating and implementing a standardized approach to business continuity management.[54]

Benefits of ISO 22301[55]

- Threat identification and assessment - discover, name, and evaluate potential serious threats to the viability of the business.

- Threat and recovery planning – so the impact and resultant downtime and recovery from real threats that do become incidents is minimized.

- Mission critical process protection –identifying key processes and taking steps to ensure they continue to operate even during a business interruption.

- Stakeholder confidence – shows prudent management planning and business resilience to internal and external stakeholders including employees, business units, customers, and suppliers.

Making Your Best Practices and Standards Selections to Inform Your IG Framework

Your organization's corporate culture, management style, and organizational goals are the enveloping considerations that must be taken into account when determining which best practices and standards should receive priority in constructing your IG framework. However, you must step through your business rationale in discussions with your cross-functional IG team, and fully document the reasons for your approach. Then you must present this approach and your draft IG framework to your key stakeholders, and be able to defend your determinations, while allowing for input and adjustments. Perhaps you have overlooked some key factors that your larger stakeholder group uncovers and their input should be folded into a final draft of your IG framework."

Roles and Responsibilities

Policies will do nothing without people to advocate, support, and enforce them. So clear lines of authority and accountability must be drawn, and responsibilities must be assigned.

Overall IG program responsibility resides at the executive sponsor level, but beneath that, an IG program manager should drive team members toward milestones and business objectives, and shoulder the responsibility for day-to-day program activities, including implementing and monitoring key IG policy tasks. These should be approved by executive stakeholders and assigned as appropriate for an employee's functional area of expertise. So, for instance, the IG team member from legal may be assigned the responsibility for researching and determining legal requirements for retention of business records, perhaps working in conjunction with the IG team member from records management (RM), who can provide additional input based on interviews with representatives from business units, and additional RM research into best practices.

CHAPTER SUMMARY: **KEY POINTS**

- **You must inform and frame IG policy with internal and external frameworks, models, best practices and standards.**
- The business user is the primary stakeholder of managed information.
- Information management is important at all stages of the lifecycle.
- Legal stakeholders can usually mandate the preservation of what is most critical, though often at great cost.
- The IGRM was developed by the EDRM Project to foster communication between stakeholders and IG adoption.
- ISO 31000 is a broad risk management standard that applies to all types of businesses.

- ISO/IEC 27001 and ISO/IEC 27002 are Information Security Management System standards.
- ISO 15489 is the international records management standard.
- The ISO 30300 series of e-records standards are managerial in nature and encourage ERM that is aligned to organizational objectives.
- ISO 38500 is an international standard that provides high-level principles and guidance for senior executives responsible for IT governance.
- ISO 22301 spells out requirements for creating and implementing a standardized approach to business continuity management.
- Your organization's corporate culture, management style, and organizational goals are the enveloping considerations for making standards and best practice selections for your IG framework.

Robert Smallwood

Part 3

Strategies & Advice from the Field

IG Education is Key to Success

Usually, securing budget for any project or program is the primary obstacle to moving forward. But that is not the case with information governance (IG) programs, according to a study of IG practitioners.

According to the IG Initiative's 2015-16 Annual Report:

> "The top barrier to IG progress is not a lack of
> money, but rather a set of factors including a *lack of
> institutional education*, communication, and leadership."

Lack of understanding/awareness of the value of IG was the highest-ranked barrier according to practitioners. This can be remedied at a modest cost with IG training courses, books and articles. Go to www.IGTraining.com for options.

The next-most cited barriers to IG progress were also rather "soft" skills: lack of communication/collaboration across functional groups, change management, and planning. These challenges can also be overcome mostly with focused directives and an investment of time, prior to undertaking the IG program effort in earnest.

The following page shows a bar chart of the Primary Barriers to IG Progress:

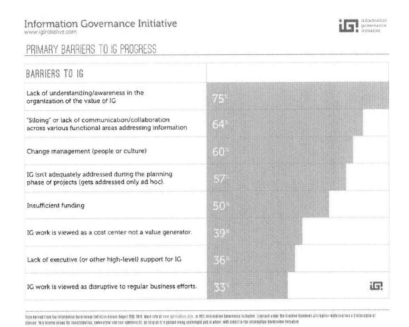

IG is a complex undertaking that requires cross-functional collaboration. And for IG programs to launch, you must cast a wide net. IG programs must have support from core IG-related functions, including records & information management (RIM), legal, IT, and information security. But a particular IG program can span across many more functional groups, including data privacy, compliance, human resources, business units, analytics, audit, and finance, according to an article published by Baron and Marcos in the October/November 2015 issue of *Practical Law.* We would add risk management and possibly knowledge management to this list.

With players from such varied functions required for IG program success, it stands to reason that they must have a common understanding of IG, a common language - its key terms, its benefits, and how the IG program will contribute to the accomplishment of the enterprise's business objectives. This means your IG steering committee must have baseline IG training to give the program a chance at succeeding.

It also means that you must pay close attention to communication and change management factors, which should be intertwined with your IG training efforts.

IG Insight: The Soft Stuff is the Hard Stuff

When organizations seek out answers for the keys to success in IG programs, they often get the typical answer from consultants and vendors: it depends.

Sure, it depends on the focus of the initial effort in an IG program. The business driver for some organizations may be cost-cutting measures that focus on reducing redundant, outdated and trivial (ROT) files to cut the cost of storage, or at least abate it.

Hard dollar savings can be made by reducing storage costs of central servers while additional savings can be gained through improved content organization (through improved taxonomy design and leveraging metadata) which lowers e-discovery collection and document review costs. That's 'hard' stuff that yields hard dollar cost savings, but it is relatively straightforward. Further, search capabilities on unstructured files such as scanned documents, Word, Excel, and PowerPoint are improved.

Other organizations are focused on reducing runaway litigation discovery costs, and concentrate their efforts on e-discovery, by not only cutting ROT and organizing e-documents, which cuts costs and improves search capabilities, but also by leveraging newer technologies such as predictive coding to automate and drastically reduce document review and costs.

Still other organizations focus their IG efforts on securing confidential information by identifying PII and protected health information (PHI) and applying security software and techniques. Using **file analysis, classification and remediation** (FACR) software finding all incidences of PII and PHI is easy, due to the unique characteristics of the data. Then various encryption tactics are applied.

And yet other organizations focus on data governance as a strong component of their IG program. Improved data governance can yield cost savings by data scrubbing, data cleansing, de-duplicating, and implementing master data management (MDM). In addition, new business insights can be gained by using data analytics, business intelligence (BI), trend analysis, and other tools. These new insights can lead to increased revenue from upselling and cross-selling existing customers, and finding new ones or creating new products or services.

The point is, there are multiple entry points for IG programs, and the focus of the effort depends on where the organization decides to invest resources. The focus of an IG program is often borne out of the greatest pain points of risk and cost that boil up to the executive suite and demand attention. After their major breach, it is taken for granted that Sony Pictures is now investing resources in identifying and securing PII, intellectual property (IP), and other confidential information.

But what do all IG programs have in common as their most critical factor to succeed? What absolutely must be done before the program has a chance to succeed?

138

It is not running FACR software to identify PII/PHI, duplicates, and out-of-date documents, and to begin broad classification of files, and insert basic metadata tags. No, that all sounds complicated but they are very straightforward processes. Simple software execution.

And it isn't implementing an **enterprise content management** (ECM) system or **enterprise file sync and share** (EFSS) aimed at reducing or eliminating shared drives and implementing a holistic approach to content management. That is what the software was designed to do. It manages content. Sure, many ECM efforts have failed but not because of the software itself lacked capability, but rather, poor implementation planning, training and communications efforts have been the primary cause.

What all IG programs must do well to succeed, the *absolute most critical elements*, are what is often referred to as "soft stuff." Soft stuff includes such activities and tasks as leadership, executive sponsorship execution, team selection and building, group dynamics, change management, communications, and training. All are critical program management functions. These are the crucial elements that any IG program must include—and do well—to succeed.

Now consider the fact that IG programs must be ongoing, so you have to plan on how you are going to keep team members motivated and performing over a span of years. How will you maintain their focus for three, four, five years or more? And instill commitment to the IG program in any team replacements or additions? These are challenging tasks. They are not easy to do, which is why many IG programs will fail, leaving careers in their wake.

As a starting point, let's examine some of the considerations for determining the best executive sponsor to drive an IG program.

What is needed is to get all the varying agendas and business objectives out on the table and to assess and prioritize them according to the organization's overall business objectives. That means nominating the most senior of the potential executive sponsors to be the executive sponsor for the IG program, with a "supporting sponsor" as backup.

So if there is a scenario where the General Counsel, CIO, SVP of Operations, and Chief Security Officer all are on board to help drive the program, perhaps the best choice is an executive who they all report up through. Say, the EVP of Risk Management. After all, risk is a key impact area for IG programs: Reduce the risk that PII/PHI is breached, reduce the risk that confidential documents or IP is breached, reduce the risk that litigation costs soar out of control and threaten the viability of the organization.

Your key players on the IG steering committee will have differing agendas and objectives. It is essential to harmonize and prioritize the objectives of the IG program to best serve the organization.

For IG programs to succeed they must get off on the right foot. That requires strong leadership and executive sponsorship, a functional and consistently motivated team, and an excellent communications and training program plan.

Easier said than done. Hopefully IG practitioners will learn from the failures in IG, ECM and records management programs and ensure that they address the "soft stuff" from the beginning.

Because it really is the hard stuff of IG.

Anticipating Conflicts in Your IG Program

There is a lot of theory in IG. The profession has been seen as "mushy" or "amorphous" but has started to firm up as case studies flow in and principles and best practices evolve. There have been many failures, although IG program efforts are, in fact, getting off the ground, expanding, and showing benefits.

However, few managers really grasp the level of planning and effort that is required to anticipate and overcome the inherent conflicts that will arise in all IG programs.

These conflicts are inevitable due to the cross-functional nature that is essential for IG program efforts. Think about it: usually the typical hierarchical organization is structured by business functions and those at the top of the ladder in C-level positions can set objectives and drive results through their direct reports. These executives are tough people who fought their way up the ladder.

However, IG programs require that these steely C-level executives from key functional areas (including Legal, I.T. Privacy, Security, Risk Management, and Records Management, and perhaps more depending on the organization) work together and collaborate.

Stop and think about that for a minute.

Consider the politics and competition that is a part of every organization. The CIO and CSO and General Counsel and others at that level are all competing to get that next promotion to Executive VP, COO or even CEO.

Competition at that level is fierce. That's why IG can be a full contact sport!

So here we have the rub, the crux of the matter, the reason why many IG programs lose steam and fail.

They are sabotaged for political purposes, often slowly and covertly, by those not leading the effort, or those who have the least to gain by its success. Since there are so many moving parts to an IG program, simple dragging of feet or missing a few meetings can start to kill the effort.

Smart and successful IG practitioners will be aware of the inherent conflicts in political agendas, business objectives, and careers, and build in conflict resolution and change management tactics into their IG program strategies.

Information Governance by Design: "Baking" IG into Everyday Processes

Information governance (IG) is a multi-disciplinary approach to secure, control, and optimize information so that information risks and costs are minimized while information value is maximized.

The goal of IG programs is to continuously strive to change the organizational culture and underlying business processes so that IG considerations including information security, privacy, e-discovery readiness, legality, records and information management (RIM) and information quality are an everyday, routine part of managing information.

Carl Thomas, the IG lead at JPMorganChase calls this process of infusing IG into business processes, the "routinizing" of IG. Once these IG considerations become a routine part of operations— "baked in" to them, you might say, the organization will have achieved, in a sense, *IG by Design*.

IG by Design means that critical privacy and security considerations and requirements become a part of everyday, routine business processes, as do regulatory and legal considerations, information quality assurance, RIM requirements, and IT efficiency considerations, all focused on maximizing information value while minimizing information risks and costs. This redesign requires deep knowledge of the organization's IG goals and strategies, and business process analysis (BPA) to redesign and streamline processes while baking in IG considerations. Then IG-enabling information technologies should be evaluated and deployed when justified and in alignment with IT strategy and business objectives. These technologies will help to monitor and enforce IG policies. Some of the IG-enabling information technologies to be considered include: business process management suites (BPMS), file analysis, classification & remediation (FACR) software, information rights management (IRM) and encryption, document and content analytics, identify & access management (IAM), enterprise search, enterprise content management (ECM), email and content archiving, legal hold notification (LHN), and others.

The result of IG by Design is reduced information, legal, and compliance risks and costs while improving information value, which leads to greater profitability and viability for the business.

But it takes vision and leadership to pull off. Most organizations are far away from the IG by Design ideal. For those just starting down the path, it is best to form business objectives, recruit an executive sponsor, and draft an IG steering committee. Then draw up the overall program and select target areas where some early wins can show real results.

If the organization's "pain point" is out of control storage costs—one client we have worked with spends $40 million/year on electronic storage costs and it is increasing by 40% each year—then file analysis tools should be tested and deployed. File analysis software can search for redundant, outdated or trivial (ROT) information and a defensible deletion/remediation strategy should be a priority. If the organization has experienced soaring attorney review costs during litigation, the focus should be on the organization's e-discovery preparation process and evaluating tools, which can dramatically cut attorney review costs, such predictive coding. If large regulatory fines have been levied for not being able to produce documentation or demonstrate that a legally defensible **records retention schedule** (RRS) is in place and followed systematically, then updating the RRS should be the focus and more employee training should be done with the business objective of reducing and eventually eliminating these fines. This process must start from the beginning with a thorough yet expedient inventorying of records, (for e-records this is done by system rather than file series according to the latest National Archives [NARA] recommendations), using all four of the methods available: 1) Observation; 2) Surveys; 3) Interviews, and, 4) Inventorying and file analysis software tools. Then records appraisal must occur to determine records values (which feeds into the retention period calculations, based on business need), and then a reasoned taxonomy design and metadata strategy, and research on regulatory requirements for retention—all of which must be considered to create an updated and complete RRS.

IG by Design as a term may be a little misleading since it implies that once the design is set, the organization has "achieved" IG. However, IG is an ongoing, "evergreen" program that evolves and expands and pushes to continuously improve.

Striving for IG by Design should be a paramount goal of any IG program. From there, with leadership, training, communications, reinforcement, solid metrics, and a prudent audit process, adjustments and improvements can continue to be made.

Don't Take On More Than the Organization Can Digest

Mark Grysiuk, CRM, CIP

In short, keep your Information Governance (IG) program simple. Your organization faces many IG challenges. Most of these challenges have often been compounded due to delay and procrastination: turning a blind eye to investing time and money in information management best practices. The result is that each day that goes by means IG problems continue to grow in size and complexity.

So now you have to react. Begin the journey to build a sustainable IG plan for your organization to compete in a world where having an established and maturing IG and information security program is a competitive advantage.

With the assumption you have obtained C-Level support, here are five recommendations:

1. **Build an IG leadership council** or committee for overseeing the implementation of a formal IG program and its ongoing operations. Key business units must be well-represented, particularly Legal, IT, Information Security, and Records Management. Keep the team intact and keep the momentum going.

2. **Identify your organization's most valued information assets and the risks posed to them.** This is critical and will require an information asset inventory. Your organization may be at the point where some initiatives must be re-prioritized so that the immediate threats are addressed in a legally defensible way.

3. **Do not make the same mistake Target Corporation made**

when it used an off-the-shelf supply chain management solution to open 133 stores in Canada, a country it had never operated in. [56]

Without a data governance strategy governed by IG Principles, Target failed to recognize that its supply chain software, which contained intricate details about 75,000 products "was riddled with flaws." There was no consistency in how young, inexperienced employees entered information into the database and no data governance "safety net" built into the software to flag potential data errors. According to the investigative team, information in the system was *inaccurate about 70% of the time*. This lead to a complete breakdown in its distribution channel because the company could not stock its shelves with the right products at the right time, driving customers away.

In early 2015, after having invested $7 billion into the expansion, the company announced that it would be filing for bankruptcy protection in Canada[57].Tens of millions in unpaid taxes and rent are owed.[58]Over 17,000 employees lost their jobs.

That case study alone is reason enough to make IG an established practice in your organization. Ask the question: What are you trying protect? The asset itself, your organization's brand and its integrity, all of the above or is it something else?

4. **Assemble a team** of information management subject matter experts and hold them accountable. Include data quality experts, data analytics experts, privacy analysts, security analysts and records management specialists as well as those in Information Technology who are responsible for maintaining the infrastructure. Each expert should have a direct line to an executive representative on the IG

leadership council with whom they can go to for support. Had Target's executives understood the risks determined by qualified IG experts, in particular those with specialized data quality management skills, more planning might have gone into its failed attempt to enter Canada.

5. **Begin to apply lifecycle management controls** on all information assets, including assigning ownership and classifying information in accordance to the sensitivity of that asset. Follow your updated Records Retention Schedule for managing the information lifecycle and controlling the volume of information. It is easy to say "everything can be protected" or that "storage is cheap." The reality is that *everything is discoverable in court* and overall storage costs are not getting cheaper due to massive and growing volumes. If there is a perception that a "back door" is available and the information is relevant to a legal matter, then courts can request it and you will have to pay for it. Not only to produce it but also perhaps in court sanctions and legal costs. Better to get rid of it in a legally defensible way then be challenged by a legal or regulatory authority.

6. **Training and communications** - Approve the planning and development of an *ongoing* enterprise-wide communications and training program. Information is the lifeblood of your business. IG training should be mandatory for all employees to protect your information assets. Training must be customized for the audience or job function.

While it is true solving this problem will require a substantial investment in time and resources it doesn't mean all of that investment must take place in the first or even the second year. Take small, incremental steps. There will be a time when some big steps will be required. Just be careful not to bite off more than the organization can digest. Good luck!

Where Do You Keep Your Crown Jewels? Identifying, Classifying and Managing Your Information Assets

By Dennis Kessler
Head of Corporate Information and Processes Division,
European Investment Bank

However we define it, the concept of "Information management" has been around for many years, steadily growing as an industry and gaining in strategic importance for organizations, seemingly without much debate or controversy.

By contrast, information governance (IG), a relatively new upstart, can appear daunting.

The reason is that there is no single recipe for success. IG is not like an IT project, with a clear beginning, middle and end. Instead, it is more like a collection of complementary ongoing activities, all designed to improve the way we manage and secure information.

And all supported by some form of governance activity, checking whether we're moving in an agreed direction in terms of standards, guidelines and metrics.

Defining IG Isn't Hard

"Information Governance" actually involves two distinct elements—instead of "Governance over information," IG is really about *"Governance over our information management activities."* It is about taking prudent care of information assets, minimizing their risks and costs while maximizing their value.

The National Archives of the UK government defines an information asset as "a body of information, defined and managed as a single unit so it can be understood, shared, protected and exploited effectively," adding that "Information assets have recognizable and manageable value, risk, content and lifecycles."

The basic concept underpinning all information management and governance activities is the idea that information has value—and so needs to be managed and safeguarded accordingly based on its value.

Organizations manage their financial assets through a combination of policies, standards, systems and governance measures. These measures aim to achieve agreed levels of oversight, scrutiny, and legal and regulatory compliance, while continuously improving.

In my experience, three key elements need to be in place for IG to flourish and deliver lasting benefits:

1. **Information principles** - these principles express the value of information and start to establish an information-focused culture in your organization.

   The principles might vary somewhat depending on the organization and industry. But they should include the following:

   - **Information is a strategic asset of the organization** - all users recognize that information is essential for the organization to achieve its mission, objectives and activities;

   - **Information belongs to the organization** - even if an info asset has an accountable owner, it still exists to benefit the organization. The "owner" is more of a steward - managing the information to ensure its quality and availability to those who need it;

   - **Information is controlled and managed** - every information asset should be managed so that we know what information is stored where, how it is used, how important it is, etc.;

- **Information is safeguarded** - according to a risk assessment of the value of the information. The more critical the information, the more stringent (and costly) should be the measures applied to protect it;

- **Information should be shared** - people must be able to find the information they need, when they need it;

- **Information has integrity** - information owners and managers follow standards and measures to ensure that the information they're responsible for is trustworthy and accurate;

- **Users understand the importance of information** and their responsibilities for maintaining and securing it.

2. **Information standards, policies & guidelines** - for information management which together describe specific behaviors, activities and outcomes needed to implement the principles and achieve the corresponding goals.

3. **Governance framework** - the structure of steering committees, roles and responsibilities and review processes which collectively asks: "How well are we meeting the principles?"

Measuring the Value of Information

In most organizations, requested spending on projects or operations requires a business case and projected "return on investment."

Although information is an asset, it's largely an intangible one, which means it's hard to put a firm dollar price on a piece or collection of information—at least in the traditional way accountants are trained to expect us to do.

Instead, think about the cost to operations, business process efficiency, customer trust and even reputation if the right information was not available to the right teams or systems at the right time.

This is exactly what information security is all about—and a good place to lay the solid foundations for effective information management and governance—even if we are unable to fund and launch a formal explicit IG program.

Although recognition of the value of IG is slowly growing, information security, and, specifically, "cyber-security" is now a firmly on the table as an agenda item for executive boards around the world. Indeed, given the widespread recent publicity resulting from industrial-scale data breaches at Sony, Target and even the US Office of Personnel Management.

Information security is now seen as an existential threat to some organizations and even economic growth (according to the World Economic Forum).

Locating the "Crown Jewels" – and Protecting Them

Once we have located an information asset, we you need to analyze and classify it to build a simple profile.

We will then store and maintain the profiles in an **information asset register**.

The term information security is based on the idea that information represents an asset which has a value.

To determine the criticality of an asset, we consider the impact of loss of the asset's:

- **Confidentiality** – has there been a breach of unauthorized access?
- **Integrity** – Can we trust the information to be accurate and complete? Has the information been tampered with or corrupted?
- **Availability** – is the information available to those people, processes or systems who need it, when they need it?

Based on its resulting criticality value, each information asset needs a corresponding level of protection - specifically, to safeguard and maintain its availability, confidentiality and integrity.

The resulting criticality value then suggests the corresponding level of protection needed to safeguard and maintain its availability, confidentiality and integrity.

Benefits of Tracking Your Information Assets

As well as greater confidence that you are protecting your information assets appropriately, this asset-based approach to managing information helps to reveal:

- Which people or teams are responsible and accountable for maintaining the confidentiality, integrity and availability of information

- Which people/teams and systems can access information, and for what purposes - whether to create, update or consume information

- How information flows and is used throughout the organization - which business processes and which decision-making points depend on which information

- Regulatory, compliance and other obligations

Practical Example

Consider the practical case of financial transaction processing system in an investment bank.

To most people, such a core and complex system is often thought of as a single entity. Stakeholders might talk about information that is "stored in the system" or "produced by the system" - as if "the system" involves a single big bucket where information is created, stored, updated and accessed.

This might be accurate when it comes to maintaining, backing-up and upgrading "the system."

However, when it comes to the distinct information assets that the system handles, the reality is more both complex—and more interesting.

- The **asset management** team will maintain records of the deals and positions representing investment decisions for customer portfolios.

- A separate **financial analysis** team might look after profit & loss statements and related reporting instruments.

- The **treasury** team will be responsible for managing treasury deals and positions.

- On the risk side, a team responsible for managing **market risk** will monitor asset prices, interest rates and related indices.

- A different risk team will track customers' **credit risk** when considering investment decisions and orders.

- On the "**back office**" side, various dedicated teams will manage data collections for account details, non-trading cash deals, settlement instructions, collateral management, and various financial instruments.

- It does not matter whether this financial jargon is meaningful or not. The point is that a single complex system can involve numerous distinct information assets, each of which has different owners and managers in different teams who might not even communicate with each other on a regular basis.

And each of these information assets will have a different profile, especially in terms of value and criticality. The highest-criticality assets should have the most stringent information security measures applied.

Only when we carry out this kind of analysis, using transparent and objective criteria, can we start to reveal where our crown jewels are located. The results are not always obvious and can be surprising – even to people working closely with the information and related systems.

To assist you in locating, describing, and categorizing your information assets and developing an information asset register, below please find a helpful set of survey questions.

Best of luck on your IG journey!

Sample Information Asset Survey Questions

1. Information Asset Description

1.1 Name: A descriptive and meaningful label for the asset

1.2 Description: What is the information asset and what it is used for

2. Ownership: This section covers the "stewardship" of the information asset, including the key roles and responsibilities of the owner and manager, together with any other stakeholders likely to be affected by the quality and availability of the asset

2.1 Owner has overall accountability for access, use and management of the asset

2.2 Manager: Hands-on manager responsible for day-to-day operations and administration. Expected to be familiar with the details of the asset content, structure and usage, and so likely to be quick to detect evidence of breach, tampering/corruption etc.

2.3 Creator: Source of the information; a person, application system or external source

2.4 Stakeholders / customers: Other stakeholders affected by the use, management, integrity or availability of the asset

3. Dates

3.1 Creation date: Date on which the asset was created (if involving a fixed lifecycle)

3.2 Last review date: Date on which the asset was last reviewed for completeness and accuracy

3.3 Date closed: Date on which the asset was closed/completed/removed from production use

4. Confidentiality

4.1 Confidentiality: Indicates the confidentiality classification of the information based on the BIS Confidentiality of Information policy (SN 1045) (NB this is distinct from the **Risk/impact Criticality** rating in section 7 below.)

4.2 Data Privacy & Protection: indicates whether the asset contains or relates to Personally Identifiable Information (PII) and potential relevance to Data Protection or Data Privacy regulations & legal risk- especially the EU General Data Protection Regulation (GDPR).

5. Retention

5.1 Retention period: Retention category (if useful – but avoid duplication and inconsistency)

5.2 System of Record: Name of the record system used to store the asset (or a subset of related business records)

6. Access & Use

6.1. Applications & Interfaces: List of applications & interfaces authorized to access the information asset, together with the corresponding access rights

6.2 User groups: List of user groups authorized to access the asset, together with the corresponding access rights

6.3 Metadata: List of any metadata needed to access or describe the context of the asset

7. Risk/ Impact of problems/issues

7.1 Confidentiality: Impact if the asset is accessed or disclosed without authorization

7.2 Integrity: Impact if the information is corrupted, tampered with or otherwise suffers a loss of integrity

7.2.1 Integrity check: Describes whether and how integrity of the information can be verified –how can we know if the asset has been tampered with or whether the asset is what it claims to be?

7.3 Availability: Impact if the information is lost or unavailable?

7.3.1 Cost / effort of replacement: Describes the cost or effort of replacing the information if it became unavailable or unusable. What business continuity plans (BCP), arrangements or implications have been identified?

Veteran Advice on Getting Your IG Program Launched

By Richard P. Kessler
Executive Director, Information Lifecycle Governance, IT Contracting and Shared Services Legal, UBS Group AG

When first developing an IG program, corporate executives should be wary to keep its initial scope narrow, carefully select the right people as its initial contributors, and create a framework that supports growth and future success.

Early "wins" are key to an IG program's long-term survival. The first IG project must be selected with care so it can be accomplished relatively quickly while also delivering demonstrable value. For example, a proposed project that requires new technology to be rapidly developed, evaluated, approved, and implemented to realize a time-sensitive, significant, revenue-generating opportunity can provide an excellent opportunity to demonstrate the value of the IG approach. In such cases, IG can be used to facilitate a coordinated, collaborative, and parallel review by SMEs within legal, litigation, compliance, operational risk, IT, HR, regulatory, and information security, and other functions that may normally work serially, separately, or worse, *at cross-purposes.* An IG program can be used to create a governance structure that coordinates these different roles. This can be a great place to start if you do not have a specific, significant, and recent incident to leverage.

If you have recently had an event that challenged your organization and perhaps resulted in damaging press or a significant drop in stock price, it often can be leveraged to start an IG program. A data security breach, regulatory fine, a lawsuit, or other significant loss, can jumpstart an IG program. It will bring together an initial set of SMEs, and serve as an opportunity for the right leader to step in and coordinate and address the incident or resulting challenge.

An experienced executive will already know how vital a dedicated, empowered, and funded senior executive sponsor is to any program. However, a fledgling program – especially an IG program – *also requires a strong, intelligent, patient, and well-spoken leader.* This person should be a subject matter expert in several IG disciplines, such as records management, eDiscovery, security, and IT, and have a working knowledge of related subject areas to enable issue spotting as challenges arise. They will need to rapidly understand and resolve conflicts and differences of opinion amongst both contributors and governance-body members alike.

The leader must also create an environment of mutual respect, understanding, collaboration, and open communication, so that minority and dissenting opinions are welcomed and no one is afraid to speak when they see an issue for their particular discipline. Foster an environment of discussion and "give and take," even if it means getting a bit off track from a meeting's purpose – this will facilitate a sense of contribution and ownership that will increase the group's effectiveness better than a rigid adherence to pre-set agendas. This same individual will then need to lead the group to a defensible and actionable decision, and create consensus for the best possible way forward. This is not easy to do, and early experiences with smaller groups will be vital so that the leader can learn from their mistakes. The process to figure out, actually "feel" out, how to manage the governance structure appropriately is an iterative one and will require patience and a willingness to adjust your approach as you go. For example, getting to a "perfect" way forward often will not be possible. A good leader will help the IG team understand that the perfect can be the enemy of the good, and that a risk-value-cost balance will often be the best achievable result.

Even with a strong leader, it is critical that the IG steering committee be comprised of strong SMEs that also have the right level of authority and responsibility within the firm. In IG, it is often all about the details, and the members of the team must understand the nuances of their field. Thus, early iterations of an IG program should include a relatively small group of stakeholders that are patient with each other, have some knowledge outside their own discipline, and can communicate well. Ideally, these people should include challengers and contributors. Diversity of opinion and perspective and the resulting challenges will help the team identify the best way forward, and contributors will help map out the path to get there.

As the scope of the IG program expands and the repeatable success becomes a reality, principles and strategic objectives of the program should be developed to serve as the constraints and guideposts for the IG team. *Creation of IG guidelines, standards, and exception procedures are vital to resolve conflicts, which will inevitably arise.* There will be times when not everyone will agree and consensus will seem unattainable; having standards and principles in place will help get and keep everyone on track.

In summary, by leveraging the right initial project or program, carefully selecting leaders and SMEs with the right mix of attributes, strong executive sponsorship, and a principled framework supporting further growth and expansion, your nascent IG program will not only get off the ground but will be poised for success and integration into every facet of your organization's change efforts.

Glossary

archive

Storing information and records for long term or permanent preservation. With respect to e-mail, in a compressed and indexed format to reduce storage requirements and allow for rapid, complex searches (this can also done for blogs, social media or other applications). Archiving of real-time applications like email can only be deemed reliable with record integrity if it is performed immediately, in real time.

ARMA

Association for Records Managers and Administrators, the U.S.-based non-profit organization for records managers with a network of international chapters.

auto-classification

Setting pre-defined indices to classify documents and records and having the process performed automatically by using software, rather than human intervention. A strong trend toward auto-classification is emerging due to the impact of "Big Data" and rapidly increasing volumes of documents and records.

backup

A complete spare copy of data for purposes of disaster recovery. Backups are non-indexed mass storage and cannot substitute for indexed, archived information that can be quickly searched and retrieved (as in archiving).

case records

Case records are characterized as having a beginning and an end, but are added to over time. Case records generally have titles that include names, dates, numbers, or places.

classification

Systematic identification and arrangement of business activities and/or records into categories according to logically structured conventions, methods, and procedural rules represented in a classification system. A coding of content items as members of a group for the purposes of cataloging them or associating them with a taxonomy.

cloud computing

Cloud computing refers to the provision of computational resources on demand via a network. Cloud computing can be compared to the supply of electricity and gas, or the provision of telephone, television, and postal services. All of these services are presented to the users in a simple way that is easy to understand without the users' needing to know how the services are provided. This simplified view is called an abstraction. Similarly, cloud computing offers computer application developers and users an abstract view of services, which simplifies and ignores much of the details and inner workings. A provider's offering of abstracted Internet services is often called The Cloud.

Code of Federal Regulations

"The Code of Federal Regulations (CFR)"annual edition is the codification of the general and permanent rules published in the Federal Register by the departments and agencies of the federal government. It is divided into 50 titles that represent broad areas subject to federal regulation. The 50 subject matter titles contain one or more individual volumes, which are updated once each calendar year, on a staggered basis."[59]

cold site

A cold site is simply an empty computer facility or data center that is ready with air-conditioning, raised floors, telecommunication lines, and electric power. Backup hardware and software will have to be purchased and shipped in quickly to resume operations. Arrangements can be made with suppliers for rapid delivery in the event of a disaster.

data loss prevention (DLP)

Data loss prevention (DLP; also known as data *leak* prevention) is a computer security term referring to systems that identify, monitor, and protect data in use (e.g., endpoint actions), data in motion (e.g., network actions), and data at rest (e.g., data storage) through deep content inspection, contextual security analysis of transaction (attributes of originator, data object, medium, timing, recipient/destination, and so on) and with a centralized management framework. Systems are designed to detect and prevent unauthorized use and transmission of confidential information.

destruction certificate

Issued once the destruction of a record is complete, which verifies it has taken place, who authorized the destruction, and who carried it out. May include some metadata about the record.

destructive retention policy

Permanently destroying documents or e-documents (such as e-mail) after retaining them for a specified period of time.

disaster recovery (DR)/business continuity (BC)

The planning, preparation, and testing set of activities used to help a business plan for and recover from any major business interruption, and to resume normal business operations.

discovery

May refer to with the process of gathering and exchanging evidence in civil trials; or, to discover information flows inside an organization using data loss prevention (DLP) tools.

disposition

The range of processes associated with implementing records retention, destruction, or transfer decisions, which are documented in disposition authorities or other instruments.

document analytics

Detailed usage statistics on e-documents, such as time spent viewing, which pages were viewed and for how long, number of documents printed, where printed, number of copies printed, and other granular information about how and where a document is accessed, viewed, edited, or printed.

document lifecycle

The span of a document's use, from creation, through active use, storage, and final disposition, which may be destruction or preservation.

document lifecycle security (DLS)

Providing a secure and controlled environment for e-documents. This can be accomplished by properly implementing technologies including information rights management (IRM) and data loss prevention (DLP), along with complementary technologies like digital signatures.

document management

Managing documents throughout their life cycle from creation to final disposition, including managing revisions. Also called document lifecycle management.

electronic document and records management system (EDRMS)

Software that has the ability to manage documents and records electronically, including physical records.

electronically stored information (ESI)

A term coined by the legal community to connote any information at all that is stored by electronic means; this can include not just e-mail and e-documents but also audio and video recordings, and any other type of information stored on electronic media. ESI is a term that was created in 2006 when the U.S. Federal Rules of Civil Procedure (FRCP) were revised to include the governance of ESI in litigation.

e-mail and e-document encryption

E-mail and e-document encryption refers to encryption or scrambling (and often authentication) of e-mail messages, which can be done in order to protect the content from being read by unintended recipients.

enterprise content management (ECM)

Software that manages unstructured information such as e-documents, document images, e-mail, word processing documents, spreadsheets, Web content, and other documents; most systems also include some records management capability.

enterprise process analytics

Detailed statistics and analysis of business process cycle times and other data occurring throughout an enterprise. This business intelligence can help spot bottlenecks, optimize workflow, and improve worker productivity while improving input for decision-making.

event-based disposition

A disposition instruction in which a record is eligible for the specified disposition (transfer or destroy) upon when or immediately after the specified event occurs. No retention period is applied and there is no fixed waiting period as with timed or combination timed-event dispositions. Example: *Destroy when no longer needed for current operations.*

Federal Rules of Civil Procedure (FRCP)—Amended 2006

In U.S. civil litigation, the FRCP governs the discovery and exchange of electronically stored information (ESI), which includes not only e-mail but all forms of information that can be stored electronically.

file plan

A file plan is a graphic representation of the business classification scheme (BCS), usually a "hierarchical structure consisting of headings and folders to indicate where and when records should be created during the conducting of the business of an office. In other words *the file plan links the records to their business context."*

Generally Accepted Recordkeeping Principles®

A set of eight Generally Accepted Recordkeeping Principles®, also known as "The Principles" within the records management community,[60] published in 2009 by U.S.-based ARMA International to foster awareness of good recordkeeping practices and to provide guidance for records management maturity in organizations. These principles and associated metrics provide an **information governance** (IG) framework that can support continuous improvement.

HIPAA

The Healthcare Insurance Portability and Accountability Act (HIPAA) was enacted by the U.S. Congress in 1996. According to the Centers for Medicare and Medicaid Services (CMS) website, Title II of HIPAA, known as the administrative simplification (AS) provision, requires the establishment of national standards for electronic health care transactions and national identifiers for providers, health insurance plans, and employers.

hot site

A hot site is one that has identical or nearly identical hardware and operating system configurations, and copies of application software, and receives live, real-time backup data from business operations. In the event of a business interruption, the operations can be switched over automatically, providing uninterrupted service.

information governance (IG)

IG is "security, control, and optimization" of information. IG is an ongoing program that helps organizations meet external compliance and legal demands and internal governance rules. IG minimizes information risks and costs while maximizing its value.

information life cycle

The span of the use of information, from creation, through active use, storage, and final disposition, which may be destruction or preservation.

information rights management (IRM)

Information rights management (IRM) applies to a technology set that protects sensitive information, usually documents or e-mail messages, from unauthorized access. IRM is technology that allows for information (mostly in the form of documents) to be encrypted and remote controlled. This means that information and its control can be separately created, viewed, edited, and distributed.

limitation period

The length of time after which a legal action cannot be brought before the courts. Limitation periods are important because they determine the length of time records must be kept to support court action [including subsequent appeal periods]. It is important to be familiar with the purpose, principles, and special circumstances that affect limitation periods and therefore records retention."[61]

long term digital preservation

The managed activities, methods, standards and technologies used to provide long-term, error-free storage of digital information, with means for retrieval and interpretation, for the entire time span the information is required to be retained.

phishing

Phishing is a way of attempting to acquire sensitive information such as user names, passwords, and credit card details by masquerading as a trustworthy entity in an electronic communication. Communications purporting to be from popular social websites, auction sites, online payment processors, or IT administrators are commonly used to lure the unsuspecting public. Phishing is typically carried out by e-mail or instant messaging, and it often directs users to enter details at a fake website that looks and feels almost identical to the legitimate one. Phishing is an example of social engineering techniques used to fool users, and it exploits the poor usability of current web security technologies.

policy

A high-level overall plan, containing a set of principles that embrace the general goals of the organization and are used as a basis for decisions. Can include some specifics of processes allowed and not allowed.

preservation

The processes and operations involved in ensuring the technical and intellectual survival of authentic records through time.

records appraisal

The process of assessing the value and risk of records to determine their retention and disposition requirements. Legal research is outlined in appraisal reports. This may be accomplished as a part of the process of developing the records retention schedules, as well as conducting a regular review to ensure that citations and requirements are current.

records integrity

Refers to the accuracy and consistency of records, and the assurance that they are genuine and unaltered.

records retention schedule

A records retention schedule spells out how long different types of records are to be held, and how they will be archived or disposed of at the end of their life cycle. It considers legal, regulatory, operational, and historical requirements.[62]

ROT

Redundant, outdated or trivial information that should be identified and deleted to improve operational efficiencies.

spoliation

The loss of proven authenticity of a record. Can occur in the case of e-mail records if they are not captured in real-time, or they have been edited in any way.

Structured information

Information that lack metadata, or has little metadata, such as email, Word documents, PowerPoint slides, scanned images, PDFs, and the like.

taxonomy

A hierarchical structure of information components, for example, a subject, business-unit, or functional taxonomy, any part of which can be used to classify a content item in relation to other items in the structure.

text mining

Performing detailed full-text searches on the content of document.

thesaurus

In taxonomies, a thesaurus contains all synonyms and definitions, is used to enforce naming conventions in a controlled vocabulary, for example, *invoice* and *bill* could be terms that are used interchangeably.

total cost of ownership (TCO)

All costs associated with owning a hardware and software system over the life of the implementation—usually considered over a range of three to five years. TCO includes implementation price and change orders (and the change order approval process), which occur when changes to the project are made outside of the original proposal. Timing and pricing of the software support fees are also critical TCO components, and may include warranty periods, annual fees, planned and maximum increases, trade-in and upgrade costs, hardware maintenance costs, and other charges.

unstructured records

Records that are not expressed in numerical rows and columns but rather, are objects such as image files, e-mail files, Microsoft Office files, and so forth. Structured records are maintained in databases.

vital records

Vital records are mission-critical records that are necessary for an organization to continue to operate in the event of disruption or disaster and cannot be recreated from any other source. Sometimes referred to as critical information assets. Typically, they make up about 3%-5% of an organization's total records. They are the most important records to be protected, and a plan for disaster recovery (DR)/business continuity (BC) must be in place to safeguard these records.

warm site

A warm site may have all (or mostly all) identical hardware and operating systems, such as a hot site does, and software licenses for the same applications, and needs only to have data loaded to resume normal operations. Internal IT staff may have to retrieve magnetic tapes, optical disks, or other storage media containing the most recent backup data, and some data may be lost if the backup is not real-time and continuous.

ABOUT THE **AUTHOR**

Robert F. Smallwood is an industry-leading author, keynote speaker, consultant, and educator. This is his fifth book on IG topics and he is the world's leading IG author and trainer. Robert is author of the pioneering text *Information Governance: Concepts, Strategies, and Best Practices* (Wiley, 2014) which is used to guide IG programs at major corporations worldwide and to teach graduated students at universities including Oxford, San Jose State, and University of Michigan. Smallwood is a founding partner of IMERGE Consulting and heads up the Institute for Information Governance. In addition to teaching IG courses, he consults with Fortune 500 companies and governments. Some of his past research and consulting clients include the World Bank, Sidley Austin LLP, Kirkland & Ellis LLP, Magna International, Tyson Foods, Johnson & Johnson, Apple, Pacific Gas & Electric, and the Supreme Court of Canada. Mr. Smallwood has published more than 100 articles, published nine books, and given more than 50 conference presentations. He is also the author of *Information Governance for Executives* (Bacchus, 2016), *Managing Electronic Records: Methods, Best Practices, and Technologies* (Wiley, 2013); *Safeguarding Critical E-Documents* (Wiley, 2012); *Taming the Email Tiger* (Bacchus, 2008) and several other books, including a novel, a theatrical play, and the first published personal account of Hurricane Katrina.

ABOUT THE **CONTRIBUTORS**

Mark Grysiuk

Mark served as editor for this book. In 2015, Mark won ARMA's prestigious Britt Literary Award and is currently serving his second two-year term on ARMA International's Content Editorial Board. He has over 14 years of experience in information management. For the past eight years he has helped organizations develop defensible disposition programs in a variety of industries, including financial services, telecommunications, government, broadcasting and technology. His specialties include electronic records management, business process analysis, and technical writing. Contact Mark via ca.linkedin.com/in/markgrysiuk/ or mgrysiuk@gmail.com.

Dennis Kessler

Dennis Kessler is an information and change management professional with more years' experience than he is willing to admit. He has worked internationally on numerous initiatives for major organizations in the banking and health sectors, in additional to several years as a business writer and editor for the Economist Intelligence Unit during ten years in Hong Kong and Osaka, Japan. After ten years as a London-based consultant, Dennis spent five years at the Bank for International Settlements in Basel, Switzerland, including two years defining and establishing information governance, before relocating to Luxembourg with the European Investment Bank.

ABOUT THE **CONTRIBUTORS**

Richard P. Kessler

Richard is responsible for Information Lifecycle Governance at UBS, serving as the Risk Controller for records management, eDiscovery, and related disciplines. He manages the Information Governance portfolio, defines and implements control frameworks, develops and communicates business requirements and standards, and is the primary liaison to Compliance and Operational Risk for monitoring and assessing Information Governance processes. For more than 25 years, he has worked in numerous IT and Legal roles, including those in enterprise architecture, application development, trade automation, and data architecture. He has also served as an ESI/eDiscovery consultant, assisting law firms and corporations with litigation readiness and response strategies.

Headquartered in Zurich and Basel, Switzerland, UBS has offices in more than 50 countries, including all major financial centers, and employs approximately 60,000 people.

INDEX

Responsible, Accountable,
  Consulted and Informed
  RACI, 66
Risk Avoidance, 72
Risk Management
  analysis and assessment, 99
  creating a risk profile, 96
  developing a mitigation plan,
    100
  ISO 31000-2009, 127
ROT, 22

S

Security Penetration Testing
  Software, 60
Sedona
  commentary on Information
    Governance, 28
Sensitive Information
  Payment Card Information
    (PCI), 68
  personal health information
    (PHI), 68
  personally identifiable
    information (PII), 68
Software
  business intelligence, 61
  Business Process Management
    Suites (BPMS), 60
  content analytics, 62
  File analysis, classification, and
    remediation, 62
  master data management, 62
  mobile device management, 61
  penetration testing, 60
  predective coding, 61
Sony Breach
  the full cost, 35
Standards
  30300
    2011, 128
  30301

  2011, 128
  Generally Accepted
    Recordkeeping Principles®,
    110
  ISO 15489-1
    2001, 127
  ISO 31000-2009, 127
  ISO/IEC 38500
    2008, 128
  MIKE2.0, 110
Strategic Planning, 103
Stream Messaging, 60
Structuring Information
  Governance Committee, 44
Survey, 57, 105, 107, 109

T

Target
  failed entry into Canada, 147
Technologies
  for implementing Information
    Governance, 58
that redundant, outdated, and
  trivial (ROT)
  the amount most organizations
    manage, 71
The Outer Ring
  IGRM. See Generally Accepted
    Recordkeeping Principles®
Three Drivers
  for justifying IG program, 72

V

Vital Records, 15

W

World Economic Forum
  Report, 22

NOTES

[1] Kerry, C. F. (2015, March 26). Lessons from the new threat environment from Sony, Anthem and ISIS. (Brookings Institution) Retrieved 2016, from Tech Tank Improving Technology Policy: http://www.brookings.edu/blogs/techtank/posts/2015/03/26-anthem-sony-isis-hack-cybersecurity

[2] http://www.cioinsight.com/it-management/inside-the-c-suite/a-modern-governance-strategy-for-data-disposal.html

[3] J. Baron & A. Marcos, "Information Governance: Establishing a Program and Executing Initial Projects" *Practical Law,* Oct-Nov 2015, p.26

[4] Ibid.

[5] Wheatley, M. (2015, February 20). Hidden costs of Sony's data breach will add up for years, experts say. (M. ". Hopkins, J. Furrier, Editors, &SiliconANGLE, Producer) Retrieved 2016, from SiliconANGLE: http://siliconangle.com/blog/2015/02/20/hidden-costs-of-sonys-data-breach-will-add-up-for-years-experts-say/

[6] J. Baron & A. Marcos, "Information Governance: Establishing a Program and Executing Initial Projects" *Practical Law,* Oct-Nov 2015, p.26

[7] J. Baron & A. Marcos, "Information Governance: Establishing a Program and Executing Initial Projects" *Practical Law,* Oct-Nov 2015, p.26

[8] Ann Cavoukian, P. (2011, January 1). Privacy by Design. Retrieved from www.privacybydesign.ca: https://www.ipc.on.ca/images/Resources/7foundationalprinciples.pdf

[9] J. Baron & A. Marcos, "Information Governance: Establishing a Program and Executing Initial Projects" *Practical Law,* Oct-Nov 2015, p.27-28.

[10] (August 2012). Mobile Communications and Records and Information Management (ARMA TR-20-2012).ARMA International.

[11] Barclay T. Blair, (2014, July 23). ZyLAB Webinar: Information Governance: 10 Things You Can Do To Get Started. Slide 10

(http://www.zylab.com/ediscovery-resources/recorded-webcasts), Accessed March 1, 2016

[12] http://ww2.cfo.com/big-data-tecnology/2015/12/why-data-needs-a-seat-at-the-corporate-table-information-governance/

[13] Barclay T. Blair, F. &. (2014, July 23). ZyLAB Webinar: Information Governance: 10 Things You Can Do To Get Started. #7 Pick Projects - for Overall Impact and For Political Capital (Accessed March 1, 2016)

[14] Ibid. Delivering Value slide, March 1, 2016

[15] Information Governance – records, risks and retention in the litigation age - See more at: http://www.aiim.org/Research-and-Publications/Research/Industry-Watch/InfoGov-2013

[16] https://www.arma.org/docs/bookstore/theprinciplesmaturitymodel.pdf?sfvrsn=2 (accessed March 5, 2016)

[17] Osterman Research, "The True ROI of Information Governance," February, 2015, p.1

[18] Ibid, p. 5

[19] Ibid, p. 10

[20] Ibid, p. 11

[21] Ibid, p. 11

[22] Ibid, p. 11

[23] Mark Woeppel, "Is Your Continuous Improvement Organization a Profit Center?" June 15, 2009, www.processexcellencenetwork.com/process-management/articles/is-your-continuous-improvement-organization-a-prof/, accessed March 6, 2016.

[24] Donald Clark, Big Dog and Little Dog's Performance Juxtaposition, "Continuous Process Improvement," March 11, 2010, www.nwlink.com/~donclark/perform/process.html, accessed March 5, 2016.

[25] Kahn, Blair, *Information Nation: Seven Keys to Information Management Compliance*, AIIM International, 2004, pp. 242-243.

[26] The U.S. Government Publishing Office (GPO), "Code of Federal Regulations," www.gpo.gov/help/index.html#about_code_of_federal_regulations.htm (accessed March 6, 2016).

[27] John Fraser, Betty Simkins (editors) "Enterprise Risk Management: Today's Leading Research and Best Practices for Tomorrow's Executives," Wiley, 2010, p. 171

[28] "ISO 31000 2009 Plain English, Risk Management Dictionary," http://www.praxiom.com/iso-31000-terms.htm, accessed March 6, 2016.

[29] John Fraser, Betty Simkins (editors) "Enterprise Risk Management: Today's Leading Research and Best Practices for Tomorrow's Executives," Wiley, 2010, p. 172

[30] Ibid.

[31] Ibid. p. 179.

[32] "Controlling the risks in the workplace" Health Safety Executive, http://www.hse.gov.uk/risk/controlling-risks.htm, accessed March 6, 2016.

[33] Project Management Institute, *A Guide to the Project Management Body of Knowledge, (PMBOK Guide),* Fourth Edition, ANSI/PMI 99-001-2008, pp. 273-312.

[34] http://www.cmswire.com/cms/information-management/the-link-between-ediscovery-and-information-governance-025867.php; http://searchcontentmanagement.techtarget.com/tip/Why-information-governance-drives-good-records-management (accessed March 5, 2016).

[35] Monica Crocker, e-mail to author, June 21, 2012.

[36] http://www.edrm.net/resources/guides/igrm Accessed March 5, 2016

[37] Kate Cumming, "Metadata Matters," in *Managing Electronic Records,* ed. Julie McLeod and Catherine Hare (London: Facet Publishing, 2005), 34.

[38]Minnesota State Archives, Electronic Records Management Guidelines, www.mnhs.org/preserve/records/electronicrecords/ermetadata.html. (accessed March 6, 2016),

[39]Charles Dollar and Lori Ashley, e-mail to author August 10, 2012.

[40]ARMA International, "Generally Accepted Recordkeeping Principles®," http://www.arma.org/docs/sharepoint-roadshow/the-principles_executive-summaries_final.doc(accessed March 6, 2016).

[41]Ibid.

[42]ARMA International, Information Governance Maturity Model,http://www.arma.org/docs/bookstore/theprinciplesmaturitymodel.pdf?sfvrsn=2(accessed March 6, 2016).

[43]http://www.edrm.net/projects/igrm (accessed March 6, 2016)
[44] Ibid.

[45]Ibid.

[47]http://www.edrm.net/resources/guides/igrm (accessed March 6, 2016).

[48] "ISO 31000:2009 Risk Management -- Principles and Guidelines" http://www.iso.org/iso/home/store/catalogue_tc/catalogue_detail.htm?csnumber=43170accessed March 6, 2016.

[49] ISO/IEC 27001:2005, "Information technology -- Security techniques -- Information security management systems – Requirements," http://www.iso.org/iso/catalogue_detail?csnumber=42103accessed March 6, 2016.

[50] ISO/IEC 27002:2005, "Information Technology—Security Techniques—Code of Practice for Information Security Management," www.iso.org/iso/catalogue_detail?csnumber=50297 (accessed March 6, 2016).

[51] "Relationship between The ISO 30300 Series of Standards and Other Products of ISO/TC 46/SC 11: Records processes and controls." White paper, by ISO TC46/SC11- Archives/records management, March 2012,www.iso30300.es/wp-

content/uploads/2012/03/ISOTC46SC11_White_paper_relation
ship_30300_technical_standards12032012v6.pdf., Accessed
March 6, 2016

[52] http://www.iso.org/iso/catalogue_detail?csnumber=51639, accessed
March 5, 2016.

[53] http://www.38500.org/,accessed March 15, 2016.

[54] ISO 22301:2012 "Societal Security – Business Continuity Management
Systems –
Requirements,"http://www.iso.org/iso/catalogue_detail?csnu
mber=50038 (accessed March 5, 2016).

[55] http://www.bsigroup.com/en-GB/iso-22301-business-continuity/
(accessed March 5, 2016).

[56] http://www.canadianbusiness.com/the-last-days-of-target-canada/
(accessed March 6, 2016)
[57] http://niagarafallsdebthelp.ca/target-files-bankruptcy-protection-
canada/March 6, 2016
[58] http://globalnews.ca/news/1790027/target-canada-owes-tens-of-
millions-in-unpaid-taxes-rent/, January 23, 2015 (accessed March 6,
2016)
[59] The U.S. Government Publishing Office (GPO), "Code of Federal
Regulations,"
https://www.gpo.gov/fdsys/browse/collectionCfr.action?collec
tionCode=CFR (accessed March 6, 2016).

[60] ARMA International, "Generally Accepted Recordkeeping Principles®,"
http://www.arma.org/docs/sharepoint-roadshow/the-
principles_executive-summaries_final.docaccessed March6,
2016). This chapter was contributed by Charmaine Brooks, CRM
of IMERGE Consulting.

[61] Government of Alberta, "Developing Retention and Disposition
Schedules," p. 122.

185

Printed in Great Britain
by Amazon